GIFTS GLITTERING AND POISONED

KALOS

The word *kalos* (καλός) means beautiful. It is the call of the good; that which arouses interest, desire: "I am here." Beauty brings the appetite to rest at the same time as it wakens the mind from its daily slumber, calling us to look afresh at that which is before our very eyes. It makes virgins of us all, and of everything—there, before us, lies something that we never noticed before. Beauty consists in *integritas sive perfectio* [integrity and perfection] and *claritas* [brightness/clarity]. It is the reason why we rise and why we sleep—that great night of dependence, one that reveals the borrowed existence of all things, if, that is, there is to be a thing at all, or if there is to be a person at all. Here lies the ground of all science, of philosophy, and of all theology, indeed of our each and every day.

This series will seek to provide intelligent-yet-accessible volumes that have the innocence of beauty and of true adventure, and in so doing remind us all again of that which we took for granted, most of all thought itself.

SERIES EDITORS:
Conor Cunningham, Eric Austin Lee, and Christopher Ben Simpson

Gifts Glittering and Poisoned

SPECTACLE, EMPIRE, AND METAPHYSICS

. . .

Chanon Ross

CASCADE *Books* · Eugene, Oregon

GIFTS GLITTERING AND POISONED
Spectacle, Empire, and Metaphysics

KALOS 3

Cascade Books
An Imprint of Wipf and Stock Publishers
199 W. 8th Ave., Suite 3
Eugene, OR 97401

www.wipfandstock.com

ISBN 13: 978-1-62032-715-9

Cataloging-in-Publication data:

Ross, Chanon.

    Gifts glittering and poisoned : spectacle, empire, and metaphysics / Chanon Ross.

    KALOS 3

    xii + 154 p. ; 23 cm—Includes bibliographical references and index.

    ISBN 13: 978-1-62032-715-9

    1. Christianity and culture. 2. Christianity and culture—History—Early church, approximately 30–600. 3. Augustine, Saint, Bishop of Hippo. 4. Liturgics. 5. Christianity—Philosophy. I. Title. II. Series.

BV178 .R67 2014

Manufactured in the USA.

for Shannon and Noah

What happens in the apparently empty ether of thought may come down to earth, and a masked metaphysics come to walk the streets—or stalk. For monsters too might float in the Empyrean, coming to earth with gifts glittering and poisoned.

WILLIAM DESMOND

Contents

Preface

This book combines contemporary philosophy, theology, and ancient Roman history. I do not remember when I first fell in love with early Christian theology, but I've always been convinced that Faulkner was right when he said, "The past is never dead. It is not even past." I first came across the concept of spectacle in Tertullian's *On Spectacle*, which was written in the late second or early third century. Many years later, after reading *Society of the Spectacle* by Guy Debord and *Empire* by Antonio Negri and Michael Hardt, I realized that the relationship between Empire and spectacle was as important today as it was in the days of ancient Rome. Over the course of many more years, I continued to connect ancient and contemporary authors until finally a coherent picture began to emerge. Some of these connections were readily apparent, and as I combed through ancient and modern texts, they seemed to leap off the page. Other connections were initially perplexing and required a great deal of thought before materializing. For example, Augustine's writings on the spectacles of Rome are almost always accompanied by his discussions of demons, but I thought that incorporating a discussion of demons into an already complex analysis of ancient and modern spectacle seemed unmanageable. However, as I read Augustine, I realized that understanding his analysis of Rome's spectacle entertainments required comprehending his interrelation of spectacle and demonic ontology. One night, after spending considerable time reading *City of God*, I was strolling through Times Square in New York. As I looked up at the glowing spectacles towering over the crowded streets, I suddenly saw what Augustine meant. The revelations of that night led to the insights described in chapter 2. This book came to be through many such surprising moments when things suddenly seemed to coalesce.

Much of the research for this book was conducted while I was serving as Director of Youth and Young Adult Ministries at Knox Presbyterian

Church in Naperville, Illinois. Knox is a large, mainline church situated in the middle of an affluent suburb of Chicago. It was a perfect place to study the relationship between consumerism, spectacle, and youth culture. Youthfulness is an essential aspect of the society of the spectacle, but, as Debord observes, the Spectacle is no friend of the young. In the Spectacle "it is things that rule and that are young, vying with each other and constantly replacing each other." The images set forth by the Spectacle have a devastating effect on the young and create a "constant antagonism between youth and adults." I witnessed this suffering firsthand in the young people I mentored. Over the course of six years, I had many conversations with young people and their parents as we endeavored together to address the challenges of living in Naperville, which sometimes seemed like the "capital city" of the society of the spectacle. It was also during this time that I began to think about the relationships between spectacle, music, and spiritual ecstasy that eventually came together as I was writing chapter 3. I am incredibly grateful for the ongoing friendships of my Christian family at Knox who continue to bless me.

I owe many thanks to many people without whom this book could not exist: first to Reverends Clint and Deb Roberts at Knox, who allowed me to serve there full time while completing doctoral work at Garrett-Evangelical Theological Seminary. The influence of their friendship and wisdom on me is evident in these pages. This book was originally a doctoral dissertation completed under the direction of Professor D. Stephen Long, who was always encouraging and patient. Studying under Steve was an extraordinarily fruitful time of learning, and I cannot begin to express my gratitude for his instruction and direction. I am equally grateful to Reverend Dr. Jason Byassee, who served on my dissertation committee and who first introduced me to many of the ancient sources that inform chapter 2. Without Jason I would surely have misunderstood Augustine and Quodvultdeus. More importantly, I am a much better person and Christian because of his friendship, and I will never cease to be challenged by the scope of his scholarship and his skill as a pastor. Before a word of this book was written much research was done, and this is because Sheri Berk, Robin Kolar, and Ginny VanBlaricom watched my son Noah for countless hours while I was in the library or the local coffee shop.

I also owe a huge debt to my friend and colleague Reverend Dayle Rounds, with whom I have the extraordinary pleasure of working at Princeton Theological Seminary. I am grateful for her consistent encouragement.

My work on this manuscript was as important to her as anything in my Princeton job description, and I am most grateful for her laughter, which got me through many long days and nights of writing. During the last five years, many Princeton friends have supported me and offered critical reflections on the manuscript and listened while I contemplated the society of spectacle. Princeton Seminary students Wendy Mohler, Michael Guyra, Todd Tracy, and Brian Tanck offered both friendship and insight. They are great scholars and pastors, and even better friends. Kenda Creasy Dean "keeps it real" and continues to help me think about the strange amalgam I have somehow managed to become: scholar, youth pastor, and seminary administrator. Pat Heran is both a friend and a colleague who humors me (more than she should have to) and helps me keep it all together. To my friends at Princeton: Charles, Seraphim, Sushama, Amy Sharon, Amaury, Shari, and Mary Beth—thanks for laughing with me.

To my parents, Bob and Kathy Ross: where did the time go? For years you have watched and encouraged me. This has been a long time coming. Thank you for your support and your love.

Finally, this book is dedicated to my lovely wife, Shannon, and to my son, Noah. It represents countless nights when Dad was not around because he was writing and reading. To Shannon: no words can express my gratitude for the support and love you have shown me over many years. You are truly the love of my life.

1

Introduction

In the twenty-first century, humanity has bumped up against the limits of the world. The processes of production and consumption that have stretched across the globe are unsustainable and often devastate the environment. Feeling the weight of this reality, the world's fourth largest city, São Paulo, Brazil, enacted legislation in 2007 to curb a massive pollution problem. It endeavored to clean the air, water, and land, and then it took an additional unprecedented step. São Paulo banned all forms of visual advertising, including billboards, signs, kiosks, and pamphlets—even the Goodyear blimp was made illegal. Despite the protests and lobbying of advertising companies, São Paulo's lawmakers were able to pass legislation against advertising because they classified the cumulative effect of mass marketing as *visual pollution*. They recognized that mass marketing is to the mind what smog is to the lungs.

Brazilian journalist Vinicius Galvao, a reporter with the newspaper *Folha de São Paulo*, described to National Public Radio's Bob Garfield the effects of mass marketing on the city before the new legislation: "São Paulo's a very vertical city. That makes it very frenetic. You couldn't even realize the architecture of the old buildings, because all the buildings, all the houses, were just covered with billboards and logos and propaganda. And there was no criteria."[1] After the legislation was enacted, Galvao observed its dramatic effect on both the appearance of the city and the outlook of its people: "You get lost now, [because] you don't have any references anymore. That's what I realized as a citizen. My reference was a big Panasonic billboard.

1. Galvao, "Clearing the Air." This interview was presented on National Public Radio's *On the Media*. In some instances I have corrected Galvao's English for the sake of clarity.

1

But now my reference is [an] art deco building that was covered . . . So you start getting new references in the city. The city's got a new language, a new identity."

Galvao's reporting showed how the removal of mass visual advertising had given São Paulo a "new language and a new identity," and he also revealed how mass marketing prevented the city from noticing a new shantytown of Bolivian immigrants. The discovery of this immigrant community became the subject of his reporting. He told Garfield, "I wrote a big story in my newspaper today that in a lot of parts of the city we never realized there was a big shantytown. People were shocked because they never saw [it] before . . . There [were] a lot of billboards in front of these manufacturers' shops, and when they were uncovered, we could see through the window [that] a lot of Bolivian [immigrants were] sleeping and working at the same place. They earn just enough for food. So it's a social problem that was uncovered [and] the city was shocked at this news." Galvao's story is a startling illustration: when a society becomes focused on consumption as a way of life, the people can see little else, especially the plight of the poor and marginalized.

In the late 1960s, philosopher Guy Debord observed that consumer society had already reached "a stage at which the commodity has succeeded in totally colonizing social life. Commoditization is not only visible, we no longer see anything else; the world we see is the world of the commodity."[2] Debord contended that the unification of consumption with social life "is the *meaning* and *agenda* of our particular socio-economic formation. It is the historical moment in which we are caught."[3] He described this historical moment as the "society of the spectacle." Spectacle facilitates commoditization by cultivating desire and shaping society in ways that make otherwise empty acts of consumption seem meaningful. The phrase "society of the spectacle" describes a consumer society in which spectacle both facilitates commoditization and becomes itself an object for consumption. It refers to "a social relation between people mediated by images"[4] that unifies social life according to the logic of an ever-expanding market.[5] The unification of spectacle with social life is relatively unnoticed unless it is suddenly removed, as in the case of São Paulo. As Debord observed, "spectacle keeps

2. Debord, *Society of the Spectacle*, 21.
3. Ibid., 9.
4. Ibid., 7.
5. Ibid.

people in a state of unconsciousness as they pass through practical changes in their conditions of existence."[6] It is neither a conspiracy of the elite nor state-sponsored control; rather, the spectacle becomes part of society and culture through the giant feedback loop that encompasses the ongoing cycles of production and consumption.

The society of the spectacle has advanced with innovations in mass media technology. In the twentieth century, mass media became the primary vehicle for increasingly sophisticated means of marketing, which constantly found new ways of unifying products with social life. Today, we live increasingly through media technologies that make living a matter of gazing. The ubiquity of screens and images in consumer culture is not accidental. Screens and images are powerful tools of objectification that render us as subjects of consumption. If a society is reduced to gazing at images of products (and images as products), then it is the culmination and ultimate fulfillment of the society of the spectacle. Although mass advertising is an important aspect of the society of the spectacle, it cannot be reduced to the manipulations of the media. As Debord observes, "spectacle interrelates and explains a wide range of seemingly unconnected phenomena. In all of its particular manifestations—news, propaganda, advertising, entertainment—the spectacle represents the dominant *model* of life."[7] Thus, the society of the spectacle is more than "mere visual deception produced by mass media technologies."[8] It is "a worldview that has actually been materialized, a view of the world that has become objective," and this worldview is "a means of unification . . . the focal point of all vision and all consciousness."[9]

Since the late 1960s, Debord's description of consumer culture as a society of the spectacle has influenced political theory, cultural theory, and theology. For example, neo-Marxist scholars like Kenneth Surin, Antonio Negri, Michael Hardt, and Slavoj Žižek have utilized and critiqued Debord's analysis of consumer culture, as have theologians like John Milbank, David Bentley Hart, and Catherine Pickstock.[10] However, neither

6. Ibid., 14.

7. Ibid., 8–9.

8. Ibid. 7.

9. Ibid.

10. In the chapters that follow, we will consider many of the ways these and other scholars have thought and rethought the society of the spectacle from their perspectives. Descriptions and analyses of the society of the spectacle appear in recent and influential volumes, such as Hardt and Negri, *Empire*; Sloterdijk, *Neither Sun Nor Death*; Milbank, *Being Reconciled*; Ward, *Cities of God*; Pickstock, "The Univocalist Mode of Production";

Debord nor the many receptions of his work have observed that spectacle is a phenomenon that our modern consumer society shares with the Roman Empire.[11] Rome's *spectacula Romana*—the spectacle entertainments held in the Coliseum and amphitheaters throughout the Roman Empire—were integral to every aspect of Rome's social life, including its politics, religion, economy, government, architecture, and entertainment. These spectacles included the gladiator fights, beast hunts, and mass executions for which Rome's Coliseum became infamous. They were the emblem of the empire's consumption and excess—the site where life itself was disposable as a means of amusement and pleasure seeking. The spectacles were prevalent throughout the empire and very popular. Early Christians were very familiar with the spectacle entertainments, but not for the same reason as the rest of the populace. Many Christian martyrs were persecuted, tormented, and killed as spectacle entertainments. Rome presented them as criminals whose refusal to participate in the cult of the emperor rendered them a malignancy that had to be publicly purged from the social body. However, in their worship and corporate life, early Christians testified to a different social reality; they represented an alternative polis and a way of living that resisted the Roman society of the spectacle through obedience to Christ.

This book recovers early Christian resistance to ancient spectacle in order to provide new and provocative insights into modern consumer culture. In the chapters that follow, ancient Christian voices echo across the centuries to reveal how the modern society of the spectacle is history repeating itself. For example, Augustine wrote much about Roman spectacles and their relationship to the demonic. By recovering his insights, we will begin to see how the modern society of the spectacle, like its ancient Roman predecessor, operates a demonic metaphysics. For early Christians, like Augustine, the sacramental logic of the Eucharist provided a metaphysical basis for resisting both Roman spectacle and its demonic metaphysics. As we shall see, the metaphysical perspective of Augustine stands in stark

---

Mitchell, *What Do Pictures Want?*; Surin, *Freedom Not Yet*; Hart, *The Beauty of the Infinite*; Ranciere, *The Emancipated Spectator*; Baudrillard, *The Perfect Crime*; Baudrillard, *The Intelligence of Evil or the Lucidity Pact*; Žižek, *Living in the End Times*; Žižek, *In Defense of Lost Causes*; Tiqqun, *Theory of the Young-Girl*.

11. One exception to this is Sloterdijk, *Neither Sun Nor Death,* 120. Sloterdijk briefly connects Debord's notion of spectacle with the spectacles of the Roman Empire, but does not elaborate significantly on the connection. He also does not discuss the way early Christians resisted Rome's "society of the spectacle" and, through the church, offered an alternative form of social life. We will consider Sloterdijk's analysis in chapter 3.

contrast to the postmetaphysical analysis of today's neo-Marxist scholars. They seek to resist the modern society of the spectacle by eschewing all manner of metaphysics, but in the course of this study, we will see why Augustine's metaphysical ontology provides a superior alternative to their postmetaphysical perspective.

Exactly how the modern society of the spectacle operates a demonic metaphysics will become clear as we explore Augustine's conception of the demonic in chapter 1 and then allow it to illuminate the spectacles of modern marketing in chapter 2. However, before delving into this and the many other insights that will emerge over the course of our study, it is necessary and helpful to provide an overview of how Roman and modern spectacle relate. We will do this by first describing the role that spectacle played in the Roman Empire. We will then examine the role it plays in the new Empire as described by Michael Hardt and Antonio Negri. This will provide a foundation for understanding how early Christianity provides insights for theological engagement with the modern society of the spectacle. Ultimately, this introduction will conclude with chapter summaries that will provide a map for the road ahead.

Early Christians and the Spectacles of the Roman Empire

As we have noted, Rome's spectacle entertainments played a significant role in every aspect of social life. Historian Donald Kyle observes, "From the emperors who took pride in the productions, to the spectators (high and low) who flocked to the shows, Romans of all classes attended, approved of, and enjoyed the games."[12] Romans used spectacle entertainments to display their social hierarchy. The front section of the Coliseum was reserved for nobles, soldiers were separated from civilians, and men sat apart from women. Special seats were given to married plebeian men and young freeborn boys and their tutors; officials wore white, whereas common people wore dark colors.[13] Patrons and producers of the spectacle entertainments

12. Kyle, *Spectacles of Death in Ancient Rome*, 3.

13. These stipulations were enacted in the first century AD. According to Seutonius, Caesar Augustus "issued special regulations to end the wholly confused and lax way of watching shows and introduced order . . . The senatorial decree provided that at every public performance, wherever held, the front section must be reserved for senators . . . Other rules included the separation of soldiers from civilians, the assignment of special seats to married plebeian men, to young freeborn boys, and close by to their tutors . . . and a ban on those wearing dark clothes except in the upper rows. Augustus confined

sat "at prominent vantage points, as citizens of status in seats of privilege, as citizen-spectators participating and sanctioning the rules and rulers of Rome."[14] This social differentiation was an important part of the enjoyment. Horace encouraged his fellow Romans to "gaze more intently on the audience itself than on the performance, since it provides by far the better spectacle!"[15] This display of social hierarchy reified the social order and gathered the people in their various stations around the spectacular displays of the empire's power. The spectacle entertainments symbolized Rome's expansion across the globe as it colonized other nations, cultures, and peoples.

Romans exhibited an insatiable appetite for both animal and human blood, which intermingled on the sandy floor of the Coliseum. At the dedication of the Coliseum in AD 80, Emperor Titus had nine thousand animals killed, and Trajan had eleven thousand killed in AD 108–109.[16] The exact number of human casualties is more difficult to calculate, but Rome had a constant supply of condemned slaves, whom it killed daily as spectacle entertainment. Seneca graphically describes the atmosphere and bloodlust in the first century AD:

> By chance I attended a mid-day exhibition [*meridianum spectaculum*] . . . now all the trifling is put aside and it is pure murder. The men have no defensive armor. They are exposed to blows at all points, and no one ever strikes in vain . . . In the morning they throw men to the lions and the bears; at noon, they throw them to the spectators. The spectators demand that the slayer shall face the man who is to slay him in his turn; and they always reserve the latest conqueror for another butchering. The outcome of every fight is death, and the means are fire and sword . . . In the morning they cried "Kill him! Lash him! Burn him! . . . Let them receive blow for blow, with chests bare and exposed to the stroke!" And when the games stop for the intermission, they announce: "A little throat

---

women to the back rows, even at gladiatorial shows, although previously men and women had sat together." Seutonius, *Aug.* 44, cited in Beacham, *Spectacle Entertainments of Early Imperial Rome,* 122–23. Moreover, Beacham observes that "Augustus was concerned not just about crowd control and decorum but also about tighter constraint over such traditional expressions of private aristocratic patronage." See ibid., 123.

14. Kyle, *Spectacles of Death in Ancient Rome,* 3.

15. Horace, *Epis.* 2.1.197–98, quoted in Beacham, *Spectacle Entertainments of Early Imperial Rome,* 126.

16. Kyle, *Spectacles of Death in Ancient Rome,* 77.

cutting in the meantime, so that there may still be something going on!"[17]

Condemned slaves who demonstrated fighting skill were sorted and
trained as gladiators. A small, select number of gladiators lived longer de-
pending on their skill and luck in the arena. Some even became famous,
though as slaves they were held captive and ultimately died in captivity.
Those not selected as gladiators were condemned as *noxii*: "For Rome, noxii
were a surplus commodity, a leisure resource, and a by-product of imperialism. They were totally at Rome's disposal, for Rome's amusement."[18] *Noxii*
suffered the torturous atrocities known as *summa supplica*, which included
crucifixion, exposure to wild beasts, and burning, and they were killed in
meridiani spectaculum, or midday spectacles, which were ritual executions.

Roman art clearly and proudly showed the killing of *noxii* on mosaics
and sculptures, which were produced for mass consumption. Kyle notes,
"Unlike the flattering, often triumphant poses of usually bloodless gladiators, condemned criminals [*noxii*] were depicted in art as helpless, terrified,
and bloody . . . *noxii* are shown nude or nearly nude, with bound hands
or bound to posts under the control of arena handlers or in the grasp of
beasts."[19]

Cicero was one of the few Romans who objected to the relentless
bloodshed of spectacle entertainments. He asked, "what pleasure can a man
of culture derive from seeing some poor mortal torn to pieces by a mighty
beast, or some fine animal impaled on the spear?"[20] However, such objections were rare among Romans, who attended the spectacle entertainments
in droves. The spectacles were popular in part because they provided a
tremendous economy. Exotic animals from as far away as Africa and India
had to be captured, transported, and kept alive. Gladiators were criminals
and slaves, but they had to be bought, trained, and fed. Merchants, called
lanistae, specialized in trading criminals (*damnati*) as gladiators, whom
they trained in gladiatorial schools. Production crews were paid to develop
and maintain the spectacle events, and the search for novel and exotic creatures to display and kill in the Coliseum took Rome beyond their borders to
new lands and peoples. The need for increasingly elaborate and spectacular

17. Seneca, *Ep.* 7.3–5, quoted in ibid., 91.

18. Kyle, *Spectacles of Death in Ancient Rome*, 92.

19. Ibid.

20. Cicero, *Ad Fam* 7.1, quoted in Beacham, *Spectacle Entertainments of Early Imperial Rome*, 64.

displays drove technological advancement and the construction of new amphitheaters and public spaces.

Because of its popularity, spectacle was integral to the political life of Rome. Funding the spectacles was the burden of Rome's politicians and officials, who utilized them to accumulate power and status. However, Roman politicians did not organize spectacles for the purpose of leisure alone. "The Roman nobles . . . perhaps more than any other social elite in history, were dependent on popular elections for the very definition of their relative status in society . . . The ultimate test and measure of *dignitas* for a republican *nobilis* was his ability to reach higher office."[21] Thus, spectacle was a two-edged sword for Rome's political elite. On the one hand, it was the source of great political power, but on the other hand, the elite had to provide the people with elaborate and expensive displays. Political careers and social status depended on the name recognition and popular opinion that spectacle provided. Thus, spectacle caught politicians in a dangerous cycle. As Beacham notes, "Not only had the character of the occasion at which games were given become more politicized, thus affecting how they were perceived and judged by the audience, but the intensified competitive element tended to express itself most directly in frequency and increased scale and sumptuousness of the presentations."[22] Both *aediles*, who were political novices, and the highest public officials were under compulsion to provide spectacle because such opulence was expected as an "important expression of the official ideology that justified, gave meaning to, and secured public support for the principate."[23]

The religious aspect of the spectacles reinforced their importance in Roman society and their effect on the populace. Extravagant parades, called *pompa* ("pomps"), preceded many spectacle entertainments. These

21. Yakobson, "*Petitio et Largitio*," 50–51, cited in Beachham, *Spectacle Entertainments of Early Imperial Rome*, 35. Although he expressed disdain for the spectacles, Cicero also saw them as an important part of Rome's electoral process; for example, during a court proceeding in which he defended a young politician named Murena, he said, "do not despise so completely the splendor of the games and the magnificence of the spectacles . . . Elections are a question of numbers and a crowd. So if the splendor of the games pleased the people, it is no wonder that this helped Murena with them. But if we ourselves . . . are delighted by the games and attracted to them, why should you be surprised at the ignorant crowd?" See Cicero, *Mur.* 38–39, cited in Beacham, *Spectacle Entertainments of Early Imperial Rome*, 15.

22. Beacham, *Spectacle Entertainments of Early Imperial Rome*, 43–44.

23. Ibid., 35.

religious processions physically connected the temple of the god or gods in whose name the spectacles were held to the spectacle venue. Symbols of gods sat in the most prestigious sections of the venue, thereby signifying their presence among the people. Moreover, funerals were celebrated as processions of spectacular *pompa* in the public spaces. The transformation and theatricalization of these public spaces during funerals coincided with the pseudo-liturgical celebration of eternal life: "The gladiatorial displays may have been in part rituals that celebrated the redemptive qualities of manly combat as well as the ability to confront and for some contestants to overcome death."[24] Beacham further notes that "visually, emotionally and psychologically, by means of the spectacle . . . the ordinary spectators' perception was modulated by and through the presence of a group of important mortal and divine guests as well as by the evocative setting of the entertainments."[25] Nothing shouted *Rome!* like the roar of fifty thousand spectators gathered in the Coliseum in the name of pagan divinity. To participate in these liturgical rituals was to have one's mind, body, and soul shaped in the image of the empire and its gods.

The Early Christian Witness

Not everyone joined in the so-called fun of Rome's spectacle entertainment. Early Christians recognized that Roman religion, politics, economics, and spectacle entertainment were not separate spheres of social life but a complex and unified matrix. Since spectacle entertainment played such a significant role in the liturgical performance of Roman paganism, and since it was integral to the spiritual formation of the entire Roman populace, Christians refrained from participating. Augustine described in *City of God* how the empire was founded on the unholy matrix of spectacle, idolatry, and material excess. He reminded Roman pagans that "the public games, those disgusting spectacles of frivolous immorality, were instituted at Rome not by the viciousness of men but by the orders of those [pagan] gods of yours . . . It was just this corruption, this moral disease, this overthrow of all integrity and decency, that the great Scipio dreaded . . . when he saw how easily you could be corrupted and perverted by prosperity."[26] Similarly, Tertullian in *On Spectacles* argued that for a Christian to participate in the

24. Ibid., 37.
25. Ibid., 27.
26. Augustine, *City of God* 1.32 (Bettenson, 43–44).

imperial spectacles was tantamount to renouncing Christ: "I shall break with my Maker, that is, by going to the Capitol or the temple of Serapis to sacrifice or adore, as I shall also do by going as a spectator . . . The places themselves do not contaminate, but what is done in them."[27]

Romans did not approve of Christians abstaining from spectacle. Tacitus considered "Christians to be guilty of 'hatred of mankind' in part because they shunned the pagan sacrifices and spectacles—the very things Romans saw as essential for integration into society."[28] When early Christians refused to acknowledge the emperor as Lord, they were condemned to death and brought into the arena to be martyred as a grotesque form of entertainment. As Kyle notes, "Christians were feared and vilified by the masses as public enemies and *noxii*: a Christian was 'a man guilty of every crime, the enemy of the gods, emperors, of all Nature together.' Slanders applied to Christians (e.g. as the dregs of society, parricides, temple robbers, religious criminials, incestuous perverts) . . . As cheap, non-bellicose *noxii*, they suffered the worst atrocities of *summa supplica*."[29]

But early Christian resistance to the empire and its spectacles was not rooted in a "hatred of mankind," as Tacitus asserted. Rather, Christian faith was the basis for a radically different vision of human society. In their shared life of worship, Christians conceived of human beings as the image of God, and in their baptismal rights, they renounced the *pompa* of spectacle entertainment and taught their catechumens to avoid the Coliseum and amphitheaters of the empire. Abstention from Rome's society of the spectacle did not isolate Christians from social life. Rather, abstention had the ironic effect of bringing them into the heart of the arena. As victims on display for the bloodthirsty populace, they became featured attractions in Rome's entertainment industry. Early Christian martyrs followed the teaching of the Apostle Paul, who wrote, "I think that God has exhibited us apostles as last of all, like men sentenced to death; because we have become a spectacle to the world, to angels and to men" (1 Cor 4:9 RSV). Christian martyrs, like Polycarp and Ignatius of Antioch, understood their martyrdoms as an opportunity to use the spectacle to perform their own public liturgy, thereby witnessing to the life, death, and resurrection of Christ.

27. Tertullian, *On Spectacles*, 83.
28. Kyle, *Spectacles of Death in Ancient Rome*, 245.
29. Ibid., 244. Kyle quotes Tertullian, *Apology* 2.16.

The Significance of Christian Witness Today

Before describing the role of spectacle in the new mode of Empire as delineated by Michael Hardt and Antonio Negri, it is important to observe how the early Christian witness situates Jesus' death and resurrection in relationship to spectacle, consumption, and politics. Pontius Pilate did not merely execute Jesus. Rather, Jesus' execution was an opportunity for Pilate to ingratiate himself with the gathered multitude who demanded, "Crucify him! Crucify Him!" Pilate quickly cast aside his initial hesitancy and concern about Jesus' innocence in favor of pleasing the bloodthirsty mob.

By offering the gift of Jesus' flesh to the gathered multitude, Pilate confirmed Rome's power over life and death. However, Jesus had foreseen the gift Pilate would make of his body and blood, and he preempted Pilate's gift with his own self-giving. Whereas the spectacle of crucifixion bids the multitude to objectify Jesus' flesh, the Eucharist invites all who would follow Jesus to participate in his death by uniting themselves with him. Thus, Jesus transformed the significance of his spectacular death by offering himself. In other words, Jesus countered the power of spectacle by making himself the object of consumption. The Eucharist is an alternative form of consumption that overturns the objectification of spectacle. Whereas spectacle maintains a critical distance between the spectator and the object to be consumed, the Eucharist unites us with Christ. In consuming the Eucharist we take Jesus' body and blood into ourselves and become participants with him in his death and resurrection.

Jesus wanted his disciples to consume him and in so doing have their desires redirected toward the goodness of God where all misguided longings can finally be satiated. Whereas spectacle misdirects and exploits desire, the Eucharist redirects it back toward its proper end, which is Christ. Through the Eucharist, Jesus' followers were no longer attracted to spectacle and endless consumption, because their desire and longing had been fulfilled by his own self-giving. Jesus' spectacular death created a New Covenant with his own blood, which became the basis for the new social order of the church. This social order *is* the body of Christ, the church, which is unified with him in the celebration of the Eucharist. The spectacle entertainments of the empire were for early Christians an opportunity to present this *true spectacle* of Christ's death and resurrection, which is the Eucharist, as an alternative form of consumption that saves misdirected desire—even bloodlust—by redirecting it toward God.

Today, Christians no longer die in the Coliseum as spectacle entertainment, but spectacle has taken new forms that cultivate unholy desires it cannot satisfy. It offers up false forms of transcendence, false gods who are unworthy of worship. Roman politicians no longer solicit the allegiance of the masses, but today we are faced with a new kind of Empire, a single logic of rule that emerges from the totalitarian power of consumption and operates in mutual relationship with spectacle. Today, the church must understand this new constitution of Empire and the role of spectacle within it in order to help the society of the spectacle become the society of the Eucharist.

Modern Spectacle and the New Empire

In recent years, Empire and spectacle have become increasingly important topics for political, philosophical, and theological discourse. In their influential book *Empire*, Michael Hardt and Antonio Negri suggest that "Guy Debord's analysis of the society of the spectacle, more than thirty years after its composition, seems ever more apt and urgent."[30] Spectacle helps explain their description of Empire as distinct from traditional, colonial power. Modern imperialism has disintegrated, but today it "has taken a new form, composed of a series of national and supranational organisms united under a single logic of rule."[31] Whereas colonial nation-states maintained their power through strictly managed boundaries of race, geography, language, currency, and cultural tradition, the new mode of Empire thrives on breaking down barriers and is infinitely adaptable. Hardt and Negri observe that spectacle thrives in this new environment because "spectacle destroys any collective form of sociality . . . and at the same time imposes a new mass sociality, a new uniformity of action and thought."[32] Spectacle "is the glue that holds together the diverse functions and bodies"[33] that regulate a sociality defined by societies of consumption. This is a much more comprehensive view of Empire than common characterizations of American power as empire.[34] Consequently, Hardt and Negri's description of Empire has become

---

30. Hardt and Negri, *Empire*, 188.

31. Ibid., xii.

32. Ibid., 321–20.

33. Ibid., 321.

34. See, for example, Gardner and Young, *The New American Empire*.

influential in many disciplines, including philosophy, political theory, and theology.[35] As James K. A. Smith observes,

> Michael Hardt and Antonio Negri make a singular contribution by providing a rigorous account of the passage to a new mode of empire that is unhooked from territories and (modern) nation-states and linked to a network of "flows" of a transnational market. Much of the theological critique of American Empire is reacting as if we lived in an age of (modern) imperialism where sovereign nation-states were the principal actors and where empires were governed from a territorial capital. But the burden of Hardt and Negri's analysis is to show that our age of empire is post-imperialist.[36]

This new mode of Empire colonizes the social imaginary and symbolic structures of culture by cultivating and shaping desire and consumption. This is due, in part, to the infinite flexibility of spectacle to colonize any culture, language, or people group. Hardt and Negri write, "There is no single locus of control that dictates the spectacle . . . As Debord says, the spectacle is both diffuse and integrated."[37]

In the days of imperial colonialism, when power was centralized in nation-states, resistance was comparatively straightforward: topple the monarchies, resist taxation without representation, create new societies, and escape to the New World. But today, where can one go to escape the new mode of Empire and the society of the spectacle? Against what can one push to resist the colonization of social life by the processes of production and consumption when their incorporation is so complete?

In response to this question, Hardt and Negri have tried to imagine a new political subjectivity that emerges from the collective power of labor and that operates independently of the vast, globalized network of Empire. They call this political subjectivity the multitude:[38] "When the multitude works, it produces autonomously and reproduces the entire world of life. Producing and reproducing autonomously mean constructing a new ontological reality."[39] However, Hardt and Negri acknowledge that resisting

---

35. See, for example, Benson and Heltzel, *Evangelicals and Empire*, and Passavant and Dean, *Empire's New Clothes*.

36. Smith, "Gospel of Freedom, or Another Gospel?" 514.

37. Hardt and Negri, *Empire*, 323.

38. For an extensive articulation of the multitude as part of Hardt and Negri's political theory, see Hardt and Negri, *Multitude*.

39. Hardt and Negri, *Empire*, 395.

Empire is no easy matter. Collective labor power may not be enough to establish and unify the multitude as a political subject against the dominance of the expanding market. They admit, "One might object at this point, with good reason, that all this is still not enough to establish the multitude as a properly political subject, nor even less as a subject with the potential to control its own destiny."[40] Moreover, the problem of unifying and mobilizing the multitude leaves them a bit perplexed: "To us it seems completely obvious that those who are exploited will resist and—given the necessary conditions—rebel. Today, however, this may not be so obvious. A long tradition of political scientists has said the problem is not why people rebel but why they do not."[41]

Debord provides insight into this perplexing quandary. He argues that a society trying to free itself from spectacle is like a religious person trying to stop believing in God. Spectacle is a power that builds upon religious sensibilities and longing for God. It focuses our gaze on a world that transcends our own immanent reality, and in this world, bodies are always young, work is easy, life is perfect, and our desires are fulfilled. Debord argues that the society of the spectacle moves the religious sensibility of heaven closer to us. Consumption takes on a transcendent, religious quality: "Consumers are filled with religious fervor for the sovereign freedom of commodities whose use has become an end in itself . . . Like a factitious god, [spectacle] engenders itself and makes its own rules."[42] This factitious god generates a different kind of mythical order where all our longings are directed toward the heaven of endless consumption, but the images and visions it proliferates are of a promised land that is always just out of reach. When consumption fails to fulfill the desire it cultivates, spectacle directs desire toward new hopes—new products—that continue the same processes in different ways.

Debord argues that the only way to resist the "factitious god" of spectacle is to free ourselves entirely from any form of religious sensibility, any longing for a transcendent world beyond our material otherness. Rather than distinguish between genuine religious worship and the religious illusion of the spectacle, he lumps all forms of religiosity together and dispenses with it all. Following Marx, Debord argues that religion is merely "the mythical order with which power has always camouflaged itself. Religion

40. Ibid.
41. Ibid.
42. Debord, *Society of the Spectacle*, 33, 14, 28.

justified the cosmic and ontological order that corresponded to the interests of the masters, expounding and embellishing everything their societies could not deliver. The spectacle is *the material* reconstruction of the religious illusion."[43] Debord further contends that spectacle is "full of metaphysical subtleties," which means that spectacle immerses us in a fictitious world constructed of our projected desires and longings that does not really exist. The alternative to this metaphysical world is a purely material world, an immanent reality grounded in the materiality of human labor power.

From the perspective of Christian theology, Debord's disdain for religion and his insistence that only immanent materiality represents reality is deeply problematic. Moreover, his likening of spectacle to religion clearly lacks nuance and theological sophistication. However, this does not mean that his analysis is unimportant or unhelpful. Despite his antagonism toward religion and lack of theological sophistication, Debord recognized that spectacle is *liturgical*—it is like the worship of a "factitious god." This insight unwittingly echoes the theology of early Christians who recognized spectacle as a form of pagan worship that coincided with the politics of Empire.

Like Debord, Hardt and Negri assume a Marxist critique of religion by contending that religion merely projects the power of labor into a transcendent world beyond. Despite their admiration of early Christianity's "new ontological basis of antagonism" toward Empire, they insist that today resistance to Empire must eschew religion and any notion of transcendence in favor of a wholly immanent ontology. They never try to reconcile the political subjectivity produced by early Christianity with their insistence that resistance can only emerge from immanent, material, a-theological processes. The multitude must embody "a material religion of the senses that separates the multitude from every residue of sovereign power and from the long arm of Empire."[44] They contend that this new religious materialism is a direct challenge to Augustine's vision of the *City of God*:

> Our pilgrimage on earth . . . in contrast to Augustine's has no transcendent telos beyond; it is and remains absolutely immanent . . . The multitude today resides on the imperial surfaces where there is no God the Father and no transcendence. Instead there is our immanent labor. The multitude interprets the telos of an *earthly city*, torn away by the power of its own destiny from any

43. Ibid.,14.

44. Hard and Negri, *Empire*, 396.

belonging to a *city of God*, which has lost all honor and legitimacy. To the metaphysical and transcendent mediations, to the violence and corruption are thus opposed the absolute constitution of labor and cooperation, the earthly city of the multitude.[45]

The chief problem with Hardt and and Negri's new religious materialism is that it tries to deny the essential religious constitution of human beings. Hardt and Negri seem to assume that religious hunger is merely imaginary, a mind trick that human society plays on itself. But religious longing is not a scheme—it is real. Human beings are made in the image of God, and they consciously and subconsciously long for connection with God. Denying this hunger merely starves the masses of much-needed spiritual nourishment. Whereas spectacle exploits human longing for transcendence by offering a poor substitute, religious materialism tries to deny the longing altogether. Spectacle fills human longing for transcendence with spiritual candy. It satisfies hunger initially, but results in malnourishment. On the other hand, it is hard to imagine how religious materialism constitutes an alternative to this malnourishment, because denying transcendence merely results in spiritual starvation. Thus, spectacle and religious materialism produce similar problems. An alternative to this spiritual malnourishment and starvation can be found in the Eucharist, which satiates our deepest longings and creates a new ontological subjectivity whereby resistance to Empire and spectacle can be realized.

Spectacle and Metaphysics

The ontological subjectivity of early Christians involved a metaphysical worldview. They recognized that the power of spectacle was not merely immanent and material, but spiritual. Although early Christians recognized that the pagan gods of Rome were mere man-made idols, they also recognized a real spiritual and demonic power behind these gods. Moreover, they observed that this power was manifested in the spectacle entertainments. In other words, they recognized that idolatry was not merely ineffectual worship; rather, it was worship that *effectively* opened the worshipers to powers and principalities that were manifested in the desires that spectacle cultivated. In order to address this metaphysical power that operated in the spectacle entertainments, they practiced ritual exorcism. In early Christianity, ritual exorcism was as important to catechesis as baptism and the

45. Ibid., 207, 396.

Eucharist. Today the tradition of ritual exorcism is still part of the baptismal liturgy in the *Book of Common Prayer*, which requires candidates for baptism to answer these three questions: "Do you renounce Satan and all the spiritual forces of wickedness that rebel against God? Do you renounce the evil powers of this world, which corrupt and destroy the creatures of God? Do you renounce all sinful desires that draw you from the love of God?"[46]

A strictly immanent ontology that precludes metaphysics, like that advocated by Hardt and Negri, does not account for spectacle as a liturgical and metaphysical power. They contend that "once we recognize our post-human bodies and minds, once we see ourselves for the simians and cyborgs we are, we then need to explore the *vis viva*, the creative powers that animate us as they do all of nature and actualize our potentialities . . . the continuous constituent project to create and recreate ourselves and our world."[47]

William Desmond questions the wisdom of thinking of human beings as self-originating, post-human cyborgs who must actualize their own potentialities apart from transcendence. He suggests, "Even when one is rationally self-determining and thus free, one is not free. Our autonomous freedom does not free us, for we are tempted to make ourselves the double of the divine and so to counterfeit God."[48] For Desmond, immanence and transcendence are mutual, each one informing the other. When human beings rather than God constitute the transcendent horizon, then mere immanence, namely the human being, is made to be transcendent in place of God. Maintaining the distinction between immanence and transcendence saves us from making ourselves God. In other words, immanence needs transcendence in order to be immanence. Maintaining a transcendent horizon requires what Desmond describes as the *art of the between,* a way of seeing humanity as situated between immanence and transcendence.

---

46. *The Book of Common Prayer,* 302.

47. Hardt and Negri, *Empire,* 92. This quotation is part of Hardt and Negri's conversation about Foucault's anti-humanism. In announcing the "death of man" Foucault was rejecting the way the transcendence of premodern religiosity was merely transferred to "Man" in secular modernity. In this sense, "post-human" refers to the absence of any kind of transcendence, whether religious or secular. Hardt and Negri follow Donna Haraway, whom they see as carrying on the work of Spinoza and Foucault in so far as Haraway "insists on breaking down the barriers we pose among the human, the animal and the machine." See ibid., 91.

48. Desmond, *God and the Between,* 13.

To occupy this space is to recognize the meaning of *meta* in metaphysics, which means in the midst yet over and above.[49] We are finite and embodied, to be sure, yet we, when we gather to worship God, are in communion with that which transcends and exceeds us. This excess of being is the beyond of metaphysics. Metaphysics recognizes the sign of transcendence without assuming a full grasp of it. Our feet never leave the ground, the practical and cultural situation of our location, yet our hands reach to the heavens. In reaching toward the beyond of metaphysics we discover what Desmond describes as the porosity of our being. When we accept our place *between* immanence and transcendence, we realize our finitude.

With this newfound humility, we begin to discern the possibility of that which cannot be adequately explained with the immanent categories of secularized social theory (sociology, psychology, cultural studies, economics, politics, etc.). Of course, social theory can be very helpful in theology, and theology should always be in conversation with other disciplines. However, secularized social theory presupposes the immanent ontology of modern foundationalism, which, as D. Stephen Long observes, "assumes true knowledge must be self-evident or incorrigibly designated by the empirical representation of a sign to an object or a valid inference from one of these two. This is a method of verification preoccupied with epistemic justification."[50] Preoccupation with epistemic justification cannot fully account for what Christians are doing when they worship God as Trinity. To pray is not merely a psychological or sociological phenomenon; it is an act of opening oneself up to transcendence. Spectacle is like a prayer offered to a malicious god. It opens us to powers and principalities; it functions liturgically, and, as Debord observes, it is full of metaphysical subtleties. Because theology does not assume the immanent categories of modern foundationalism, it is uniquely situated to understand spectacle as a malicious metaphysics, the evil of idolatrous worship.

William Desmond observes that "evil sometimes seems unloosed with a life of its own, outside our best good will and power. It seems to have a power disproportionate to anything attributable to the evil we undoubtedly originate."[51] But understanding and articulating this sensibility—that we produce evil yet evil somehow exceeds us—requires metaphysics. Desmond

---

49. Desmond develops the porosity of being in a trilogy of books: *Being and the Between*, *Ethics and the Between*, and *God and the Between*.

50. Long, *Speaking of God*, 12.

51. Desmond, *God and the Between*, 331.

further contends, "Even if we make some sense of moral evil by attribution to our will, the issue is evil relative to creation, not just the human creature. Does the story of the Fall name the malignancy, the sometimes demonic energies unloosed, energies other to human will? There seems evil in excess of the moral evil we can impute to any human agent. Do we invoke a more than human agency? There seems no a priori reason to rule this out."[52] However, it is hard to begin a conversation about metaphysics "with the words 'post-metaphysical' being bandied about with all the assurances of the self-evident . . . Politically minded people delight in the realism of their reminding the metaphysical dreamers: this all is here and now, not over there, all to be done now with feet on the ground, not with heads in the clouds and with longing for somewhere over there, a nowhere other world."[53] However, those who turn a blind eye to metaphysics fail to realize that metaphysics entails political and practical manifestations. Spectacle is the glittering and poisoned gift of an idolatrous liturgy, a malicious metaphysics that is produced by us, yet also transcends us and colonizes social life.

But how do we discern the metaphysical aspects of the glittering yet poisoned spectacles? Consider the atrocious violence of Rome's spectacle entertainments. For most modern readers, the torture, bloodshed, and brutality of these spectacles are unimaginable and revolting to think about. As Kyle remarks, "Modern scholars have long pondered how civilized Romans could condone and even enjoy, make sport of, watching hundreds and even thousands of humans and animals being killed in elaborate public spectacle."[54] Yet the overwhelming majority of Roman society

52. Ibid., 257. My italics. This is *not* the same as the argument for radical evil, which ascribes ontology to evil itself. I am arguing for the perspective of traditional Christianity articulated by Augustine, which has always held to evil as privation and to an understanding of Satan as a fallen creature: "[T]he Devil was once without sin . . . sin first came into existence as a result of the Devil's pride . . . the Devil is the Lord's handiwork. For there is nothing in nature, even among the last and least of the little creatures, that is not brought into being by him, from whom comes all form, all shape, all order; and without those definitions nothing can be found in nature or imagined in the mind. How much more must the angelic creation derive from him" (*City of God* 11:15, Bettenson 447). Satan is not evil in himself; he was created good but rebelled against God. In his rebellion he is still dependent on God, and his only ability is to pervert and distort the good of creation. This is very different from the Kantian tradition of "radical evil," which conceives of evil as possessing being in and of itself and operating independently of God. For the genealogy of radical evil including its Kantian roots, see Milbank, *Being Reconciled*.

53. Desmond, "Neither Sovereignty nor Servility," 156.

54. Kyle, *Spectacles of Death in Ancient Rome*, 5.

enthusiastically attended and gloried in the spectacle entertainments. To-day we ask, "How is this possible?" but we can also put this question to contemporary society's spectacle entertainments. For example, interactive video games are exceedingly violent and graphic.[55] Players assume the role of an avatar who engages in graphic acts of extreme violence, murder, pros-titution, drug use, drunk driving—in the words of one user, "anything you could want!"[56] The common defense of such games is that they are just fantasy. When the player assumes the role of the character in the game, he is merely wearing a mask and pretending to be someone else. But as Slavoj Žižek observes,

> wearing a mask can be a strange thing: sometimes, more often than we tend to believe, there is more truth in the mask than there is in what we assume to be our real self. Think of the . . . per-son who, while playing a cyberspace interactive game, adopts the screen identity of a sadistic murderer and irresistible seducer—it is all too easy to say that this identity is just an imaginary supple-ment, a temporary escape from his real life . . . The point is, rather, that since he knows that the cyberspace interactive game is just a game, he can show his true self, and do things he would never do in real-life interactions—in the guise of fiction, the truth about himself is articulated.[57]

The excuse that the game is just a fantasy is a way of deceiving ourselves. The debate about whether such realistic, simulated violence in video games encourages real violence misses the more glaring question of why the player *enjoys* acting out such horrors in the first place. How does such desire come to reside *in his being*?

55. There are many examples of such games. Consider *Grand Theft Auto IV*, which Guinness World Records deemed "the most profitable entertainment release of all time, far surpassing other video games, film, and book releases"; according to the Guinness World Records website, *Grand Theft Auto IV*, which was released in spring 2008, sold "3.6 million units and earned $310 million in its first day of release, earning Guinness World Records for the Highest Grossing Video Game in 24 hours and the Highest Revenue Generated by an Entertainment Product in 24 hours" (http://www.ign.com/articles/2008/05/13/grand-theft-auto-iv-breaks-guinness-world-records-with-biggest-entertainment-release-of-all-time). For a similar account of *Grand Theft Auto IV*'s ri-valing major entertainment films, see National Public Radio, "New 'Grand Theft Auto' Game Shakes up Hollywood," transcript, May 9, 2008, http://www.npr.org/templates/transcript/transcript.php?storyId=90323103.

56. National Public Radio, "'Grand Theft Auto IV' Arrives in Stores," transcript, April 29, 2008, http://www.npr.org/templates/story/story.php?storyId=90024836.

57. Žižek, *Iraq*, 146.

Metaphysics helps us discern how perverse desire becomes part of a person's being by displacing desire for goodness, truth, and beauty. When distorted desires become part of our being, we are in the grip of powers and principalities that tear at our souls. Of course, the player of the video game may hardly recognize what has happened to him since, as Žižek points out, he can rationalize his desire as mere fantasy. In the society of the spectacle, we are encouraged *not* to question our desires but to accept and liberate them; consumption is the supposed key to freedom and happiness. But when we confuse mere liberation of desire with truly desiring goodness, truth, and beauty, we trade freedom for bondage. This invisible bondage is in some ways worse than physical bondage, because it controls us from within. We are possessed by powers that misdirect our longing for God toward things unworthy of the image of God—*which is what we are.* Although our desires may be misdirected, they signify our need for communion with transcendence. Even the horrors of bloodlust and violence, whether enacted on the floor of the Coliseum or through the virtual reality of a violent video game, are an opportunity to become aware of our misdirected longing for God. At the heart of the society of the spectacle is a voracious appetite for more, which only God can satiate.

Chapter Summaries

The chapters that follow will explore some of the areas in which spectacle cultivates misdirected desire for God, including bodies, violence, and images. In each chapter, we will mine the riches of early Christians who were witnesses of an alternative to the society of the spectacle. We will bring these ancient insights to bear on the many ways in which modern spectacle operates as an idolatrous liturgy.

Chapter 1, "Rome's Politics of Consumption and the Early Church," further explores the significance of Christ's crucifixion within the context of Rome's spectacle entertainments. After providing more detail about the connections between spectacle and Roman politics, we will read Jesus' crucifixion in light of the politics of Judea in the first century. Despite his initial resistance and interest in Christ's innocence, Pontius Pilate quickly caved to the demands of the Jewish leaders and offered Jesus up as a spectacle entertainment. This chapter will begin to develop the significance of the Eucharist as a gift that draws humanity into a different kind of consumption and gathers us for alternative community and public witness.

For early Christians, Christ's example was both the source and resource of their resistance to spectacle. After a close reading of Augustine's account of Alypius in Rome's Coliseum, we will dig deeper into the ways the early church during Augustine's time resisted spectacle through catechesis, exorcism, baptism, and Eucharist. Augustine explicitly described Christ as the "True Spectacle" on whom Christians should set their gaze. We will also consider the connection between spectacle and idolatry, which Augustine described as the worship of demons. Roman paganism regarded demons as mediators between immanence and transcendence and deemed them worthy of worship because of their perfect, immortal bodies. Augustine argued that Christ was the True Mediator between humanity and divinity, and he taught that the worship of demons reflected a malformed desire for the worship of the True God.

Chapter 2 brings the important insights of chapter 1 to bear on the modern society of the spectacle. After assessing the relationship between modern democracy and the society of spectacle and describing how spectacle degrades the classical Citizen Subject of modern democracy, we will look at the role that images play in advertising and their power to shape and form society. Like Roman spectacles, the spectacle of advertising plays an important role in the cultivation of desire and formation of consumer subjectivity. We will consider the relationship between the images of ancient idolatry and the spectacles of modern advertising. Whereas the modern tendency is to think of idolatry as ancient and superstitious, we will show how idolatry functions in the society of the spectacle and corresponds to the double consciousness of the image. Augustine's description of idols shows how the spectacles of modern advertising subject consumers to a demonic metaphysics, especially in the way they displace real bodies with idealized bodies that occupy a space between immanence and transcendence. These bodies appear continually in advertising and in other aspects of the society of the spectacle, and they are designed to cultivate the demonic passions of the soul in consumers. Finally, we will move from an analysis of advertising and entertainment to ask how early Christian resistance to spectacle and Empire can inform the search for a new political subjectivity. Whereas Marxist theorists like Antonio Negri, Michael Hardt, and Kenneth Surin articulate a purely immanent ontology and forswear the role of transcendence and metaphysics, we will articulate how early Christians constructed a political subjectivity in resistance to Empire through the metaphysics of the Eucharist and Christian worship. The Eucharist is the template for a

Christian metaphysics that teaches the Christian to see the world not as a collection of consumable and usable objects but as gift.

Chapter 3 further unveils the metaphysical operation of the society of the spectacle by exploring the relationship between spectacle and ecstasy. Through Thomas Aquinas's twofold account of ecstasy as either intellective or debasing, we will contrast the Eucharist and consumer culture. Thomas describes how the gift of the Eucharist corresponds to an intellective ecstasy that draws the Christian believer into a higher state of both love and understanding. It does this by piercing his being in order to create a new and deeper bond with the object of love who is Christ. This experience of intellective ecstasy maintains the priority of the intellective appetite over the sensual appetite. The society of the spectacle, on the other hand, enflames the sensual appetite and thereby subjects a person to the pathos of his lower desires. It does this through popular entertainment, advertising, violence, and other means.

After exploring Aquinas's account of ecstasy, we will consider how Roman spectacles cultivated debasing ecstasy. This is apparent in the writings of Augustine and Seneca, and after analyzing their accounts, we will use Aquinas to illuminate Christ's crucifixion as a spectacle of debasing ecstasy. This analysis of debasing ecstasy in Roman spectacle will be juxtaposed with the ecstasies of the modern music festival. The modern music festival is one of the world's greatest spectacle entertainments, and, as we shall see, the spectators at these concerts and shows often exhibit profound experiences of ecstasy.

As we examine both Roman and modern spectacles, we will see how debasing ecstasy exhibits a misguided longing for God. For as Thomas Aquinas said, a human being "must, of necessity, desire all, whatsoever he desires, of the last end . . . And if he desire it, not as his perfect good, which is the last end, he must, of necessity, desire it as tending to the perfect good, because the beginning of anything is always ordained to its completion."[58] Through Thomas's account of ecstasy, it becomes possible to see how the debasing ecstasies manufactured in consumers by the society of the spectacle are actually deep but misdirected yearnings for God. The sacramental logic of the Eucharist over-accepts debasing ecstasy and transforms it into communion with God. The recipient of the Eucharist looks at the world differently—not as a consumer for whom all things are means to selfish ends, but as a person who has received a gift of immeasurable grace. He

58. Aquinas, *Summa* I-II, 1 cited in Williams, *Ground of Union*, 94.

has exchanged debasing ecstasy for what John Milbank describes as the relational ecstasy of Christ's forgiveness. This ecstasy of forgiveness lifts him to a higher knowledge of himself (an intellective ecstasy) as a creature made in the image of God.

2

Rome's Politics of Consumption and the Early Church

> When I was a young man . . . I thoroughly enjoyed the most degrading *spectacles* put on in honor of gods and goddesses . . . Who could fail to realize what kind of spirits they are which could enjoy such obscenities? Only a man who refused to recognize even the existence of any unclean spirits.
>
> —AUGUSTINE, *CITY OF GOD*[1]

In the days of the empire, Rome's ruling elite realized that spectacle entertainment was a powerful political tool for shaping popular opinion and accumulating political power. In their pursuit of prestige and wealth, Roman emperors and officials created such a strong desire for spectacle entertainment that consuming it became integral to Roman culture, religion, politics, and economics. The first part of this chapter describes the relationship between Roman politics and spectacle and situates the crucifixion of Jesus of Nazareth within this context. Understanding Jesus' crucifixion as spectacle sheds new light on the significance of the Eucharist as an alternative to a society formed by conspicuous consumption.

The second part of this chapter considers how Augustine of Hippo engaged the problem of spectacle as a theologian and pastor. Augustine understood spectacle's influence on his congregants because he, too, had been

---

1. Augustine, *City of God* 2.4 (Bettenson, 51–52). My italics.

an enthusiastic spectator. Augustine understood spectacle as a demonic ontology that cultivated insatiable desire in spectators, and through his preaching and teaching, Augustine encouraged those seeking membership in the church to have their desires converted by Christ, the "True Spectacle." He also utilized the catechumenate to help those seeking baptism in the church recognize how spectacle had come to possess and corrupt their desires. The catechumenate redirected the catechumens' desires to consume the Eucharist as the true longing of the human soul. In the early Church, the catechumenate was a process of cleansing the spiritual palates of those preparing for baptism, and today, examining the ancient catechumenate helps us recover the importance of spiritual cleansing for the efficacy of the Eucharist.

Ultimately, this chapter provides a reading of Jesus' crucifixion and a recovery of the early Church's relationship with ancient spectacle that will be brought to bear on the modern society of the spectacle in chapter 3. Like Rome's spectacle entertainments, modern spectacle cultivates desire and directs it away from God towards consumption, which cannot satisfy humanity's longing for God. Today, as in the days of early Christianity, the Eucharist can be understood as an alternative form of consumption.

Part I: Spectacle, Politics, and Consumption in Imperial Rome

Spectacle and Politics in Imperial Rome

Immediately following Julius Caesar's death in 44 BC, Mark Antony and Octavian were locked in a bitter rivalry for power over Rome. As the adopted son of Caesar, Octavian had received the promise of a considerable inheritance from Caesar and the funds to administer Caesar's spectacle entertainments, the *ludi Victoriae Caesaris* (the games of Caesar's victory). The right to administer these spectacle entertainments publicly displayed Octavian as Caesar's successor and provided him the means of winning the goodwill of the masses. He understood well that the spectacle entertainments were the key to shaping public opinion and launching his political career. However, Octavian was caught in a political predicament because his rival, Mark Antony, controlled Caesar's funds and refused to release them. Since he could not access his inheritance, Octavian risked everything by selling all his property and borrowing enormous sums to provide the needed spectacle entertainments and enter Roman political life. He quickly became a prominent politician and general who eventually established himself as Caesar Augustus, the first emperor of Rome.[2]

Augustus' use of spectacle to accumulate power and status is a quintessential example of how "ambitious politicians went to great lengths to display their status and enormous expense to distribute generosity [in the form of spectacles] when it was politically expedient."[3] Violent spectacle entertainments had become an increasingly important part of Roman social life and politics over the course of several centuries. The first gladiatorial shows in 264 BC featured three pairs of contestants, and by 174 BC there were thirty-seven pairs. Games held by Julius Caesar in the first century BC increased the number of pairs to 320, and Agrippa held spectacles featuring more than 700.[4] Spectacle entertainments involving gladiators were called *munera,* meaning "gift" or "offering." The term *munera* originated in the era of the Republic and denoted funeral rituals conducted to commemorate publicly the death of an important individual: "[T]he idea was apparently that the death of a slave was owed to the dead person or to the gods of the underworld."[5] Beacham notes that in their early inception *munera* "served as a collective celebration of courage and fighting skill, as well as a demonstration of the power these had to overcome death."[6] But as the Roman Republic became an empire, the direct link between funerals and *munera* weakened, and *munera* came to signify a celebration in the name of one or more gods. They were often associated with an emperor's triumph over his enemies. Thus, the religious sacrifice of physical bodies—both human and animal—demonstrated his power and religious devotion publicly.

Although spectacle was a powerful political tool for Rome's ruling elite, they did not employ it at their leisure. Their political careers and social status depended on the name recognition and popular opinion spectacle provided. In the later Roman Republic and during the empire, spectacles "had become an indispensible instrument for political advancement . . . no *nobilis* aspiring to reach the highest offices could ignore the possibility that he would need the votes of what to him must have been the lowest dregs

2. For a description of the important role spectacle played in Octavian's rise to power, see Beachham, *Spectacle Entertainments of Early Imperial Rome,* 93.

3. Ibid.

4. Plass, *Game of Death in Ancient Rome,* 51.

5. Mahoney, *Roman Sports and Spectacles,* xiii.

6. Beacham, *Spectacle Entertainments of Early Imperial Rome,* 14.

of the city populace."[7] Because of this political pressure, the Roman elite took extraordinary financial and social risks to surpass one another. Cicero expressed concern about one young aspiring *aedile* named Titus Annius Milo: "He is preparing to give the most magnificent games, at a cost that has never been exceeded by anyone . . . it is his private estate that I am afraid for, and now he is beyond mad since the games he is going to give will cost a million sisterces."[8] Such opulence was expected as an "important expression of the official ideology that justified, gave meaning to, and secured public support for the principate."[9] Not just *aediles* but the highest public officials were under extreme compulsion to provide spectacle. In their pursuit of power, wealth, and status, Roman politicians became increasingly dependent on spectacle as a means of cultivating popular opinion, and the populace increasingly demanded spectacle of leaders. This was especially the case after the fall of the Republic and the advent of the empire.

More than anyone before him, Augustus recognized the political importance of spectacle entertainment, and as emperor he created their first formal administration. Augustus and the emperors who followed him were proud of the magnitude of death and suffering displayed in the spectacles they sponsored. Augustus boasted that his spectacle entertainments featured more than ten thousand gladiators and deaths of more than thirty-five hundred animals. Dio Cassius reported how Emperor Trajan exceeded Augustus's example: "Upon Trajan's return to Rome . . . he gave spectacles on 123 days, in the course of which some 11,000 animals, both wild and tame, were slain, and ten thousand gladiators fought."[10] Spectacle entertainments encompassed a variety of activities, including theatrical presentations and circus events, but the most dramatic spectacles were the violent *munera* (gladiatorial fights), *venationes* (animal hunts), and the torture of common criminals, called *noxxi*. Augustus organized these violent spectacles into a tripartite system: mornings featured beast shows and animals hunts, the

7. Ibid., 3.

8. Cicero, *Ad Quint. Frat.*, cited in Beacham, *Spectacle Entertainments of Early Imperial Rome*, 72.

9. Beacham, *Spectacle Entertainments of Early Imperial Rome*, 128.

10. *Dio Cassius* 68.15, quoted in Futrell, *Roman Games*, 35. Kyle notes that generally, over time, the spectacles grew in number of days and victims. There were 65 days of games under Augustus, 93 under Claudius, and 135 under Marcus Aurelius. These spectacle entertainments included a variety of events such as gladiator fights and ritualized executions. See Kyle, *Spectacles of Death in Ancient Rome*, 77.

noon hour featured elaborate executions of *noxii*, and the mid-afternoon featured gladiators.[11]

Fully understanding Rome's bloody spectacles requires recognizing their relationship to religion and human sacrifice. In ancient cultures, religious worship was a powerful way of socializing and establishing a body politic, and Augustus utilized this connection between spectacle and religious worship to his political advantage. His administration of spectacle coincided with a revitalization of pagan religion.[12] He built eighty-two new temples and initiated a comprehensive refurbishment of many other temples, including the temple to Apollo. Augustus linked the temple directly to his house via a ramp from its forecourt, and he instituted a quadrennial spectacle honoring Apollo. Beacham observes that "Augustus and the imperial family functioned not simply as revered leaders but also as dynamic emblems that attracted and inspired deep patriotic and religious sentiment . . . he encouraged the worship of his divine spirit through the cult of the Numen Augusti, which provided an outlet for Romans to express their religious feeling [for Augustus] in a beneficial fashion without 'proclaiming his full divinity, but [leaving] the possibility that he was indeed divine wide open for posterity to decide.'"[13]

Rome's gods and spectacle entertainments were literally and symbolically connected by a religious procession, called the *pompa*. Futrell describes how "the spectacle itself began with the *pompa*, a procession that included political and religious elements as well as the performers at the games."[14] This procession included a platform that was "typically a means of transporting the images of the gods and the deified emperors that were a standard part of the *pompa*."[15] The *pompa* paraded the bodies of gladiators, *noxii*, and beasts to be sacrificed before the whole populace and surrounded them as sacrificial objects with a religious aura. It featured placards (*tituli*)

11. For more on Augustus' formal administration of spectacles, see Kyle, *Sport and Spectacle in the Ancient World*, 297–98.

12. Futrell observes, "The Imperial goal of assimilating provincials made use of the arena as a sacred space . . . Augustus made clearest use of the amphitheater as an integral part of the Imperial Cult, in the earliest phase of emperor worship. The amphitheater encouraged a large number of participants to join in the celebration of the central authority, thereby confirming the divine status of the emperor and legitimizing his rule" (*Blood in the Arena*, 5–6).

13. Beacham, *Spectacle Entertainments of Early Imperial Rome*, 113.

14. Futrell, *Roman Games*, 87.

15. Ibid.

that distinguished gladiators from *noxii* and identified the official who was to be credited with providing the gift of their sacrificial deaths.

Augustus encouraged his political subordinates to follow his example of consolidating power through spectacle entertainments, and through his sponsorship spectacle became an increasingly important part of the expansion of the empire and colonization of the provinces. Rome's amphitheaters and spectacles were "more than just a fancy building, more than a place for expensive, bloody games; they represented a social and political institution central to the Roman Empire. The basic function of the amphitheater was as a tool of Romanization, not merely in terms of its outward form, specific to the Roman world, but as pertains to ideas, concepts, and overall impact."[16] The unity of spectacle and religion provided a powerful mechanism for assimilating provincial peoples. It was an especially important means of socialization in the early empire when emperors and governors were establishing Roman authority among many cultures. In the province of Judea, Augustus subsidized spectacles given by King Herod the Great, the puppet king of the Jews, to celebrate the institution of his new capital in 10/9 BC. Herod, in turn, dedicated it to Augustus and planned to hold them quadrennially.[17] This created a strong and very public bond between Herod and Augustus. For Herod's spectacles, "Augustus personally supplied everything needed for the shows and Livia [his wife] also donated a large amount of money. Herod himself provided lodging and entertainment for the great number of official guests. With imperial subsidization . . . Herod promoted Augustus' image and expansive games policy."[18]

In an unruly province like Judea, where the Jews consistently resisted Roman rule, the judicial facet of spectacle was an especially important aspect of asserting Roman authority. To maintain order, a first-century governor like Pontius Pilate could utilize spectacle to display his power publicly. By making a spectacle out of the suffering and death of the individual, the Roman ruler emphasized his own power and superiority. Public displays of death as a form of entertainment dramatically reinforced the image of the emperor and his representatives as the givers and takers of life: "From

16. Futrell observes that Romans built major amphitheaters independent of urban centers. In creating amphitheaters and spectacle, "Greater weight was given to the projected sociopolitical impact either in quelling potential unrest or in incorporating non-Roman peoples into the Roman worldview" (*Blood in the Arena*, 5).

17. Kyle, *Sport and Spectacle in the Ancient World*, 294–95.

18. Ibid., 295.

the time of Augustus on, various forms of executions were performed on an increasingly spectacular basis . . . The victim's lasting agony and death provided a terrifying and exemplary public spectacle . . . under the Empire the torture and aggravated death of criminals became a standard part of *munera* [gladiatorial spectacles]."[19] Kyle observes that "for Rome both the killing, as a performance, and the disposal [of bodies] as a display, were to be *seen*."[20]

Execution as public spectacle involved the demonization and alienation of Rome's enemies. Whereas tragic violence can evoke feelings of sympathy and compassion, spectacle violence marginalizes the victim and displays him as an abomination and object of ridicule. Throughout the amphitheaters of the empire, hundreds of thousands of people took great pleasure in the suffering of those whom the state had condemned as criminals or enemies. Futrell observes, "When the victim is demonized or alienated from the empathy of the audience, the viewers identify instead with the perpetrators of violence, gaining an intense feeling of satisfaction, even joy, in their vicarious revenge upon the victim."[21] Whether the spectacle was a condemned gladiator fighting to his death or the prolonged suffering of someone on a cross, the spectators reveled in the so-called pleasure of spectacle: "Feeling morally superior and distant, the spectators showed no humanitarian sentiment or sympathy. Crowd reactions were ones more of pleasure than revulsion, amusement rather than terror."[22] This co-participation in the condemnation of the criminal reinforced the social perception of Rome's authority. For example, when Pontius Pilate in Judea crucified Jesus of Nazareth as a political insubordinate who had claimed to be the King of the Jews, the spectators took great pleasure in his suffering; as they watched him die, they mocked him and hurled all manner of insults against him, and thus implicitly underscored Rome's rule.

Pilate and the Spectacle of Jesus' Crucifixion

Pilate was appointed by Emperor Tiberius as governor of Judea in about AD 26, and according to Josephus, he remained there for ten years, leaving

---

19. Ibid.

20. Ibid., 160.

21. Futrell, *Roman Games,* 49.

22. Kyle, *Spectacles of Death in Ancient Rome,* 54–55.

in AD 36.[23] The position of governor of Judea was not a highly regarded one, primarily because the Jews were difficult to govern. The Romans had taken direct control of the area only twenty years earlier and were still trying to understand this unruly and strange population. Pilate's predecessors had not stayed long, and so Pilate was already the fifth prefect of Judea. Tensions between the Jews and their Roman governors were so strained that Pilate's immediate predecessor, Valerius Gratus, had taken to subduing the Jews through mass crucifixion.

Spectacle entertainment may have been a welcome diversion for Pontius Pilate. In her lucid study of Pilate, Anne Wroe speculates, "If Pilate was a true Roman, the hours spent in the circus at Caesarea—entering to the crowd's applause, throwing out coins among the spectators . . . might well have been the happiest aspect of his job."[24] Administering spectacle entertainment reinforced a positive relationship between a governing official such as Pilate and the people he ruled. As governor, Pilate would have needed to secure the necessary facilities and resources for spectacles. Wroe notes how he "would need to get wild panthers, keeping them in cages to judge their sinuous stretching and the thrilling flash of their fangs. He would need to recruit gladiators and worry about their morale . . . Chariots would have to be built, horses trained."[25]

When Pilate arrived in Judea, he wanted to display his absolute authority as the ruling representative of the emperor, and one of his first acts was intended to make this clear to the Jews by displaying the Roman standards in Jerusalem. The standards were the sign of his authority as appointed governor, but Pilate's predecessors had conceded and agreed not to display the Roman standards on the walls of the Antonia fortress in Jerusalem; instead, the standards were dismantled and left in the guardroom in Caesarea. But when Pilate sent troops to Jerusalem for garrison duty, he ordered them to carry and display the standards upon arrival. They did so under the cover of darkness, so that when the Jews entered the city on the next day, the standards were already in place, proudly displaying the authority and power of the new governor.

However, Pilate had much to learn about his new subjects and their religious obstinacy. According to Josephus, a few days after the displaying of the standards, Pilate awoke to a huge crowd of Jews outside his palace

23. See Wroe, *Pontius Pilate*, 61–62.

24. Ibid., 69.

25. Ibid.

in Caesarea who had marched there from Jerusalem—more than sixty miles—to petition the removal of the standards.[26] Pilate was not about to back down and lose his first confrontation with his subjects, and so the new governor became locked in a standoff with the determined crowd of Jewish protesters. Finally, after five days, Pilate ordered them into the Great Stadium of Caesarea. This move was symbolic since the stadium would have been the site for spectacle entertainments, including the likely execution (and torture) of dissidents. But when Pilate had his soldiers draw their swords, the Jews did not fight but fell prostrate; they preferred death at the hands of Pilate's men to transgressing the law of God. Faced with the consequences of ordering a massacre and the inevitable creation of martyrs, Pilate relented. Wroe observes that this was Pilate's "first defeat, and perhaps the hardest to take. Not only the emperor's honor had been at stake, but his own ability to keep order and impress Roman ways on his province. His humiliation so delighted the Jews that they appointed a new feast day, the third of Kislev, to commemorate the day 'when the standards were taken away from the pavement of the Temple.'"[27]

In the wake of this debacle, Josephus tells us that Pilate made another unpopular decision when he decided to build an aqueduct. Water was difficult to find in the Judean dessert, and inhabitants of Jerusalem and the surrounding areas had to build great reservoirs and expend much energy to capture rainwater. Pilate's aqueduct was impressive by Roman standards and stretched over twenty-four miles, and in other provinces of the empire the people would have applauded a great aqueduct of this sort. However, Josephus wrote that the Jews "were not pleased with what was done about the water" because it was financed with *corban*.[28] *Corban* was sacred money sent to Jerusalem by the Jewish Diaspora, and Pilate had no authority to use *corban*; he probably struck a deal with the Jewish leadership, likely Caiphas, the high priest, to gain access to this sacred money. The Jewish leadership was equally guilty of using *corban* to fund dubious endeavors, including the thirty pieces of silver given to Judas for his betrayal of Jesus. When Judas tried to return the money, it was refused because it was no longer ritually pure (Matt 27:3–6).

---

26. For Josephus' description of this event, see *Wars of the Jews* 2.9.2–3, in *Works of Josephus*, 609.

27. Wroe, *Pontius Pilate*, 105.

28. Josephus, *Antiquities of the Jews* 18.3.2, in *Works of Josephus*, 480. See further description in Josephus, *Wars of the Jews*, 609. See also Wroe, *Pontius Pilate*, 106.

Eventually, the tensions over Pilate's use of *corban* erupted in violence. During one of his trips from Caesarea to Jerusalem, a large gathering of Jews protested, forming an imposing ring around his tribunal. Pilate, having learned from his previous experience, prepared for this possibility by dressing his soldiers in Jewish garb. Appearing as common people, the soldiers infiltrated the angry mob undetected and carried daggers and swords beneath their robes. Finally, when Pilate had had enough, he signaled to his men, who carried out a horrific massacre of the assembled crowd, killing many and chasing the survivors all the way to the steps of the temple. Wroe suggests that this show of brutal force may have been what Luke meant when he described Jesus being asked about "'the Galileans whose blood Pilate had mingled with their sacrifices.' Perhaps within the holy place [of the Temple], certainly outside it, Jewish blood was on the flagstones and smeared along the walls. How much water from the new aqueduct would it take to wash them clean?"[29] Josephus described the Jews as "so sadly beaten, that many of them perished by the stripes they received, and many of them perished as trodden to death, by which means the multitude was astonished at the calamity of those that were slain and held their peace."[30]

Conflicts with Pilate did not pacify the Jews for long. Though Pilate wielded the sword, the Jews recognized that Pilate was vulnerable in that his success as governor was contingent on their peaceful submission and the payment of taxes. Emperor Tiberius expected Pilate to ensure the stability of Judea and the smooth flow of funds to Rome, and Pilate's engaging in violent conflict with the Jews risked the stability of the province and ultimately his political career. The Jews exploited Pilate's precarious political situation when he decided to display gold shields in Herod's palace in Jerusalem. The Herodians strongly objected and insisted on their removal because these were consecrated shields, the kind "hung up in public building or in the temple of the god who had been prayed to and had answered the prayer."[31] For the Herodians, the shields were idols, and Philo says that they objected to Pilate, saying, "Tiberius is not desirous that any of our laws or customs shall be destroyed. And if you yourself say that he is, show us either some command from him, or some letter, or something of the

---

29. Wroe, *Pontius Pilate*, 109.

30. Josephus, *Works of Josephus*, 609.

31. Wroe, *Pontius Pilate*, 110.

kind that we . . . may cease to trouble you."[32] This resistance placed Pilate in a difficult situation since removing the shields, which had been publicly dedicated to Emperor Tiberius, would offend the emperor's honor and display Pilate's weakness before the Jews. On the other hand, a Jewish revolt would enrage Tiberius even more, and in this instance the Jewish populace was empowered by the powerful Herodian princes. According to Philo this "exasperated [Pilate] in the greatest possible degree, as he feared they might in reality go on an embassy to the emperor."[33] Recognizing his precarious situation, Pilate backed down and removed the shields from the Temple, thus exhibiting his weakness.

The most famous contest between Pilate and the Jewish leaders is the crucifixion of Jesus of Nazareth. Jesus was arrested and delivered to Caiaphas, who, according to John's Gospel, "had advised the Jews that it was better to have one person die for the people" (John 18:14). Caiaphas and the Sanhedrin condemned Jesus to death, but because they lacked authority to administer capital punishment, they had to convince Pilate of his guilt. This turned out to be a difficult task because of the political tension that existed between Pilate and the Jewish leaders. In order to convince Pilate to sentence Jesus to death, they argued that Jesus was guilty of sedition, of claiming to be the "King of the Jews" (Matt 27:11; Mark 15:2; Luke 23:3; John 18:29–38); in Luke's Gospel, they further accused Jesus of forbidding payment of taxes to Caesar.

However, concern from the Jewish leaders over the welfare of the Roman Empire was wholly insincere, and Pilate recognized that the charges against Jesus were designed to pressure and manipulate him. Naturally, Pilate resisted the Jewish leaders and ascertained that Jesus represented no real threat to Rome. He further discerned that "it was out of jealousy that the chief priests had handed him over" (Mark 15:10; cf. Matt 27:18) and subsequently pronounced Jesus innocent of the charges brought against him, saying, "I find no basis for an accusation against this man" (Luke 23:4; John 18:38). Wishing to avoid any unnecessary participation in Jewish affairs, Pilate delegated the matter to Herod. Though Herod treated Jesus with contempt, he ultimately returned him to Pilate, whereupon Pilate declared Jesus' innocence: "You brought me this man as one who was perverting the people; and here I have examined him in your presence and have not

32. Philo, *On the Embassy to Gaius*, in *Works of Philo*, 784.
33. Ibid.

found this man guilty of any of your charges against him" (Luke 23:14–16; cf. John 18:38).

However, Pilate's intention to release Jesus never materialized because of the pressure placed on him by the crowd, which had gathered for a special Passover custom involving the release of a prisoner. Releasing captives was a means for Roman officials to cultivate popular opinion by showing mercy, and it was common at certain festivals such as *lectisternia* and *bacchanalia*.[34] Albinus, who succeeded Pilate as governor in Judea, once displayed his benevolence by releasing all condemned criminals. Pilate's custom of releasing a prisoner during the celebration of Passover was likely intended to demonstrate his benevolence before the huge crowds that gathered in Jerusalem. It would have been a way for him to recognize the religious and cultural importance of the celebration: release a prisoner from bondage at Passover just as the Jewish people were released from bondage in Egypt.[35] When the crowd solicited Pilate "to do for them according to his custom" (Mark 15:8), Pilate asked them about Jesus: "Do you want me to release for you the King of the Jews?" (Mark 15:9; cf. Matt 27:17, John 18:39). However, the chief priests and Jewish elders had already "stirred up the crowd to have [Pilate] release for them Barabbas instead" (Mark 15:11). They recognized that Pilate could not disregard the crowd, so they "persuaded the crowds to ask for Barabbas and to have Jesus killed" (Matt 27:20). Initially, Pilate maintained Jesus' innocence before the crowd, asking, "Why, what evil has he done?" (Matt 27:23; Mark 15:14; Luke 23:22; cf. John 19:4), but the crowd "*shouted all the more, 'Let him be crucified!'*" (Matt 27:23; Mark 15:14, emphasis added). Finally, when "Pilate saw that he could do nothing, but rather that a riot was beginning," he publicly washed his hands before the crowd and declared himself innocent of Jesus' blood (Matt 27:24). Then he "released Barabbas for them; and after flogging Jesus, he handed him over to be crucified" (Matt 27:26).

Early Roman law clearly prohibited officials from condemning a person according to the will of the people: "The *Law of the Twelve Tables*, which Pilate, as a magistrate, was meant to have read, made this quite clear: 'When they want to absolve a heinous crime or condemn an innocent man, the crowd's empty voices must not be listened to.'"[36] However, by the first

34. Wroe, *Pontius Pilate*, 247.

35. Ibid.

36. Ibid., 248–49.

century BC, Cicero had lamented that "no one learns that law nowadays."[37] For a Roman official such as Pontius Pilate, who oversaw an unruly province, spectacle provided a means of focusing social tension—including frustration with the ruling governor—on a scapegoat. Kyle writes, "Under obligation to provide expiations and entertainments, officials condemned the lowly or the defenseless . . . damnation provided emotionally satisfying results [for the spectators] . . . Rome was seeking spectacle resources for diversions, but it was also seeking expiation and scapegoats for imperial problems. It was trying to cleanse itself."[38] Spectacle was a politically savvy means for a governor like Pilate to redirect the social frustrations of a mob on the verge of a riot, especially during the tense week of Passover. Consuming spectacle entertainment distracted the populace from its economic difficulties and frustrations with the government and placed the sponsoring ruler in a favorable light.

However, the people's appetite for spectacle could undermine the authority of a ruler, as it did in the case of Pilate. Ultimately, Pilate's concern for justice was eclipsed by the crowd's desire to consume Jesus' body and blood as spectacle. Pilate was willing to resist the Jewish leaders who had brought Jesus to him, but when faced with the crowd's demand for a crucifixion, Pilate's resolve crumbled. Like other politicians, Pilate was greatly influenced by the appetites of the people he governed. As Wroe observes, "Even Caesar . . . would feel curiously weakened and afraid that the fawning throng would turn on him. With a small group of men you could talk rationally; but the crowd had to be harangued at maximum volume, with sweeping gestures, and in the process all subtlety of thought would disappear . . . Only the most primitive ideas could get through; ideas requiring a yes or no. You roared into the answering roar."[39]

Spectacle, Consumption, and the Politics of the Eucharist

Jesus had journeyed to Jerusalem knowing that it would result in his crucifixion. Wroe suggests that for Jesus "the form was vital: and so was the sheer spectacle, the showiness, of crucifixion. Jesus meant to be on display, so that his death could have its cosmic effect. 'When you have lifted up the Son of

37. Ibid.
38. Kyle, *Spectacles of Death in Ancient Rome*, 101–2.
39. Wroe, *Pontius Pilate*, 249.

Man, then you will know that I am he,' he said once. Another remark was possibly even more specific: 'If I am lifted up from the earth, I will draw all men unto me.'[40] Jesus meant his crucifixion as an invitation drawing people into the kingdom of God. He celebrated this invitation with the meal of the Eucharist, where he invited his followers to partake of his body and blood.

The Eucharist can also be understood in contrast to the gladiator's *cena libera* and *sacramentum*. On the day preceding a spectacle, gladiators were put on public display "for anyone who cared to view them" and provided with a banquet (*cena libera*).[41] This meal was a "ritual device to turn lowly, vile human sacrificial victims into worthy, noble sacrifices."[42] The bodies of gladiators were further sacrilized through an oath called the *sacramentum*. As members of a gladiatorial *familia*, they swore to be "burned by fire, bound in chains, to be beaten, to die by the sword."[43] Barton observes that the gladiators' sacramental meal was simultaneously devotion, consecration, and execration on the eve of death.[44] It prepared the gladiator as a spectacle to be consumed, a gift of the ruling elite to the masses. In preparation for his own imminent death, Jesus of Nazareth served his own sacramental meal, saying, "This is my body, broken for you, and my blood poured out for you." With these words Jesus became both *the ruler who gives and the one whose body is given*. By unifying these roles in himself, he gave the spectacle of his crucifixion a particular meaning. His death would signify the rule of God rather than the power of Rome and its ruling elite.

It is also helpful to understand the Eucharist as a stark contrast to the elaborate feasts associated with Rome's spectacles. Whereas Roman emperors and politicians spread lavish banquets, and offered up the bodies of gladiators and crucified *noxxi* for the crowds, Jesus laid before his disciples a simple meal and offered up his own body.[45] The distribution of food before and during spectacles was a powerful political tool that tied Rome's political leadership to the people they ruled. For example, Statius praised the way Emperor Domitian's spectacles gathered all classes of people around a

---

40. Ibid., 163. Cf. John 12:32.

41. Kyle, *Spectacles of Death in Ancient Rome*, 82.

42. Ibid.

43. Ibid., 87.

44. Barton, "Savage Miracle," cited in ibid.

45. See Plutarch, *Moral Essays* 1099B, and discussion in Futrell, *Roman Games*, 86–87. See also Kyle, *Spectacles of Death in Ancient Rome*, 82.

common meal: "Every class eats at the same table: children, women, plebeians, knights, senators: freedom has relieved respect. Even you yourself are here at the banquet like one of our company. Which of the gods has leisure for this, or would undertake such a thing? Now everyone, poor or well-off, prides himself on sharing a meal with our leader."[46] Kyle observes that "Cicero (*Off.* 2.57) complained that aediles squandered money on 'public banquets, doles of meat among the people, gladiatorial shows, magnificent spectacles, and wild beast fights,' but he knew that such things were politically advantageous."[47] During spectacles, Roman politicians distributed gifts, called *missilia* or *lots*, to people in the stands. The gift might be fruit or other food, or it might be tokens, which the spectators could later exchange for food. Dio describes how Emperor Titus celebrated a one-hundred-day spectacle in AD 80 in which he "threw down into the Coliseum from aloft little wooden balls variously inscribed, one designating some article of food . . . or again horses, pack-animals, cattle or slaves. Those who seized them were to carry them to the dispensers of the bounty, from whom they would receive the article named."[48] Similarly, Domitian distributed nuts, dried fruit, and cakes, showering them on the spectators by means of a rope stretched across the amphitheater.[49] These "mass scramblings," which were called *sparsio*, were a powerful political mechanism that enabled the common people to participate in the conspicuous consumption engaged in by the wealthy, ruling elite. Kyle observes that "people were not just passive spectators: they interacted with their leaders and became players in a communal sporting drama. Tokens perhaps assigned to spectators the meat of a particular beast being killed before their eyes. The spectacle was a free-for all communal contest. You had to catch the objects, animals, or tokens. You had to participate to win."[50]

Plass describes the combination of mass feeding and mass destruction of bodies as "conspicuous consumption" and "commodification." Moreover,

---

46. Statius, *Silvae* 1.6, cited in Mahoney, *Roman Sports and Spectacles*, 62.

47. Kyle, *Spectacles of Death in Ancient Rome*, 191. The practice of using spectacle entertainments to distribute food antedated the Roman Empire. Kyle writes, "In 328 BC, M. Flavius distributed a dole of meat to those who walked in his mother's funeral procession. Livy, 8.22.2–4 says that the meat caused Flavius to win the tribuneship" (*Spectacles of Death in Ancient Rome*, 205 n. 66). See also Veyne, *Bread and Circuses*, 220–21.

48. Dio 66.25.4–5, cited in Kyle, *Spectacles of Death in Ancient Rome*, 191.

49. See *Suet. Dom.* 4.5, Dio 67.4.4., in Kyle, *Spectacles of Death in Ancient Rome*, 191.

50. Kyle, *Spectacles of Death in Ancient Rome*, 192.

he observes that "the rate or scale of consumption became an index of symbolic values" for Roman culture and society. The Roman historian Dio described spectacle as the vast expenditure and use of resources, including the expenditure of human life, by using the verb *analisken*. Plass argues that *analisken* is best translated as "consumption," because it "introduces a special way of looking at death in the arena."[51] He says, "The implicit commodification brings to mind the revealing use of 'waste' . . . In lending itself to extravagance, consumption acquires a broader, symbolic social meaning beyond considerations purely of quantity."[52] Feasting, material excess, and the expenditure of human life were all integral to spectacle entertainment, and they played a role in organizing Rome's social order around conspicuous consumption. Writing in the first century AD, Statius described the sheer excesses of Roman spectacle thus:

> Something noble from the Pontic nut trees, or dates from Idyme's mountains, the plums that good Damascus grows on its branches, the figs that ripen at Ebussus or Caunus—all these fall abundantly, free for the taking. Little people-cakes, sweetmeats, pastry from Amerina—not overcooked!—wine flavored wedding cakes, and stuffed dates from hidden palms were falling . . . loosed upon the Roman people in the amphitheater. Jupiter may send clouds all over the world and threaten the broad fields with rain, if only our own Jupiter will keep up *this* rain . . . As the crowd murmurs at its new delights, they also take pleasure in watching. There stand the weaker sex, untrained with swords, nonetheless taking on a manly fight . . . Over there see the bold order of dwarfs, whom nature has made short and gnarly. They deal out wounds and threaten death at each other's hands—such hands! Father Mars and bloodthirsty Virtue laugh! Who can sing of the spectacles, the unrestrained laughter, the parties, the free banquets, the broad river of wine? Now even I flag and, drunk on your wine, am dragged off at last to sleep.[53]

In the simple meal of the Eucharist, Jesus provided an alternative to conspicuous consumption and spectacle. Jesus accepted the will of the

---

51. Plass, *Game of Death in Ancient Rome*, 47.

52. Ibid. In describing spectacle in terms of consumption, Plass cites Dio 60.13.1–2. Plass writes, "Dio, in fact, uses just that notion. When people were thrown to the beasts, 'few animals but many humans died this way, some fighting each other, others eaten by animals . . . that is how he [Emperor Claudius] used them up [*analisken*]" (47).

53. Statius, *Silvae* 1.6, quoted in Mahoney, *Roman Sport and Spectacles*, 63.

crowd to make him a spectacle and turned the horror of the cross into the means of human salvation. In other words, he took the desire to consume his body and blood as a spectacle and gave it a different meaning in the form of the Eucharist: "Take and eat. This is my body broken for you; my blood shed for you." Rather than block or refuse the ill-formed desires of the crowd who called for his crucifixion, Jesus overaccepts their malformed desire to consume and presents himself as gift.[54] The one who accepts this gift and consumes Jesus' body and blood as Eucharist is no longer a gazing spectator, but a participant in his death and grateful recipient of a gift. The difference between the crowd, who consumed Jesus' body and blood as spectacle, and the disciples, who consumed him as eucharistic gift, is the nature of the consumption and the desire of those who partake. Whereas spectacle merely perpetuates desire toward insatiable consumption, the Eucharist directs desire toward participation in the death and resurrection of Jesus.

Rome's ruling elite formed Roman society around conspicuous consumption, but the Eucharist introduces a different kind of ruler, a Messiah and King of the Jews. Whereas Rome's rulers found themselves compelled to sacrifice the bodies of *others* (animals, gladiators, and *noxii*) to emphasize their authority over life and death, Jesus of Nazareth, the Christ, offered *himself* as a sacrifice. To eat the body of Christ was to *become* the body of Christ; it was to be incorporated into a new body politic. Roman rulers recognized this new political society as a threat to their social order, and they subsequently persecuted Christians just as they had persecuted the Messiah; Christians became spectacles, scapegoats and objects of disdain.

However, early Christians recognized that martyrdom in the empire's amphitheaters was an opportunity to proclaim the gospel. Robin Darling Young observes that Christian martyrs willingly accepted their fate as spectacle entertainment and subsequently used the spectacle for their own purposes: "The martyrs knew well what they were dealing with. They were opposing their sacrifice to the sacrifices of the local and universal cults of Rome, and opposing their visions of true imperium, derived from Jewish scripture, to the accepted order of those who ruled the Mediterranean and surrounding lands."[55] Early Christians conceived spectacle as an

54. I am indebted to Samuel Wells for my understanding of overaccepting. Wells develops the notion of overaccepting as a Christian strategy for engaging evil in his *Improvisation.*

55. Young, *In Procession Before the World,* 8.

opportunity to witness to Christ by going "in procession before the world."
Young says,

> Martyrdom was a spectacle played on the terms of Graeco-Roman
> society. Romans were, notably, devoted to public games, which
> were also violent spectacles. Christian communities invaded those
> spectacles and turned them to their own purposes as athletes in
> games they did not invent, and as officiants in sacrifices they set up
> against the sacrificial civic religion of the Romans. Christian com-
> munities became (at least in their own view) the victors in court
> cases and dramatic spectacles where logically they had no hope
> of persuading or triumphing . . . they for the first time provided
> victim-victors who came from the lower classes, or who were
> women. Now these people became, through their explicit identifi-
> cation with Christ, not criminals or refuse but acting subjects, that
> is to say, persons.[56]

When Christian martyrs went "in procession before the world," they understood themselves as offering the gift of the gospel to Roman society.
Christian martyrs effectively opposed this false, idolatrous gift by offering
the *true gift* of God—the Eucharist. Young observes, "When the Eucharist
was still private, not open to non-Christian view, the martyrs' sacrifice was
public and dramatic . . . Martyrdom was also understood . . . as a sacrifice
parallel and similar to Christ's passion and the Eucharist, that is to say, as a
redemptive sacrifice."[57]

For example, when Ignatius of Antioch was condemned to death in
the arena, he offered himself as an object of consumption, as food for wild
beasts. In this, according to Young, he "has already described himself in
Eucharistic terms" by following the example of Christ, who offered his own
body and blood. Young contends that Christian martyrs followed the example of Christ in offering themselves figuratively as "food not only for the
benefit of their own communities, who enjoy God's favor and a good future
in exchange, but for their persecutors as well."[58] In his letter to the Romans,
Ignatius wrote, "I am the wheat of God, and let me be ground by the teeth
of the wild beasts, that I may be found the pure bread of Christ."[59] In this
text Ignatius wants his death to be an alternative sacrifice that provided the

56. Ibid., 9.
57. Ibid.
58. Ibid.
59. Ignatius, *Letter to the Romans*, ch. 4.

spiritual food for his own community and an offering for the spectators that redirected their desire to consume toward the desire to partake in the Eucharist. Moreover, he sees his own salvation as coming through a shift in desire away from the "worldly vanity" and "pleasures of this life" glorified by spectacle entertainments toward the "the bread of God." He writes, "And now, being a prisoner, I learn not to desire anything worldly or vain . . . there is no fire in me desiring to be fed; but there is within me a water that lives and speaks, saying to me inwardly, Come to the Father. I have no delight in corruptible food, nor in the pleasures of this life. I desire the bread of God, the heavenly bread, the bread of life, which is the flesh of Jesus Christ, the Son of God."[60] In wanting to partake of the flesh of the Son of God made available in the Eucharist, Ignatius points to Christ as the true and right object of our desire that unites us with the society of the church and God's kingdom, an alternative to Rome's society of the spectacle.

Part II: Spectacle and Eucharist in Augustine

Spectacle as Perverse Eucharist in Confessions

Spectacle entertainment was popular in North Africa and especially in Carthage. Augustine of Hippo was intimately familiar with Rome's spectacle entertainments. In his Confessions, Augustine described the intoxicating power of spectacle by relating the experiences of his friend Alypius. His account of Alypius' experience reveals how spectacles effectively cultivated wicked desire in individual spectators, and it demonstrates how spectacle became a mass phenomenon that shaped Roman social life and politics.[61]

Augustine writes that "the whirlpool of Carthaginian immoral amusements sucked [Alypius] in; it was aboil with frivolous shows, and he was ensnared in the madness."[62] Although Augustine recognized the harm that spectacle inflicted on his friend, he did not initially confront Alypius "about his reckless addiction to worthless shows, or attempt to save him from ruining his fine intelligence on them." However, this changed one day when Alypius recognized himself in Augustine's description of spectators

60. Ibid.

61. Fagan considers Augustine's description of Alypius an important account of the psychosocial effects of spectacle on individuals and in Roman society. See Fagan, Lure of the Arena, 1–12.

62. Augustine, Confessions (Boulding, 143). Subsequent quotations in this section are from the same volume, 145–47.

as "enslaved by that craze." In light of Augustine's teaching, Alypius decided to stop attending the spectacles: "With a strong resolve of temperance he shook his mind free, and all the filth of the circuses dropped away from him. Never again did he go there." However, during a trip to Rome, Alypius found himself under "an entirely unexpected craving for gladiatorial entertainments." He did not want to attend the spectacle, but his friends and fellow students "happened to find the stadium open to them, and as is the way with close friends, drew him in by force, despite his vehement protests and struggles." Alypius resisted them, saying, "You may drag my body into that place and fix me there, but can you direct my mind and my eyes to the show? I will be there, and yet be absent, and so get the better both of you and of the performance."

Once inside the amphitheater, Alypius maintained his resolve, "keeping the gateways of his eyes closed, forbidding his mind to go out that way to such evils." However, his determination was not enough: "At a certain tense moment in the fight, a huge roar from the entire crowd beat upon him. He was overwhelmed by curiosity, and on the excuse that he would be prepared to condemn and rise above whatever was happening even if he saw it, he opened his eyes and suffered a more frivolous wound in his soul than the gladiator he wished to see had received in his body." Spectacle ignited desire and passion in Alypius: "As he saw the blood he gulped the brutality along with it; he did not turn away but fixed his gaze there and drank in the frenzy, not aware of what he was doing." Alypius' desires carried him away and he lost himself. "No longer was he the man who had joined the crowd; he was now one of the crowd he had joined, and a genuine companion of those who had led him there." Moreover, he became an evangelist for the spectacles, one who was "lured back again . . . dragging others."

Augustine recognized a connection between gazing spectacle and consumption. Augustine tells us that when Alypius "*saw* the blood he *gulped* the brutality . . . he *fixed his gaze* there and *drank in* the frenzy." Augustine describes Alypius as consuming a perverse Eucharist; spectacle provided him with the blood of a sacrificial victim, but it was not the blood of Christ. His participation did not unite him with the society of the church but with Rome. A similar observation appears in *On the Government of God* by Salvian, a Christian theologian and contemporary of Augustine. Salvian compared the consumption of victims by beasts with the spectral gaze of the crowd. He remarked, "the greatest pleasure [of the spectacles] is to have men die . . . to have the bellies of wild beasts gorged with human flesh; to have men eaten, to the great joy of the bystanders and the delight of onlookers, so that the victims seem *devoured* [*devorari*] almost as much by *the eyes* of the audience as by the teeth of beasts."[63]

Gazing and Consuming True Spectacle

Augustine's church was full of people who, like Alypius, had been corrupted by spectacle. They had been attracted by the allure of a false Eucharist and had set their gaze on the blood of a sacrificial victim who was not Christ. This situation posed a very significant pedagogical challenge for Augustine and other early Christian leaders.

One Sunday, shortly after Christmas, Augustine looked out at a relatively low attendance for morning worship. Weeks before his church had been full of people celebrating Advent and Christmas, but now the throngs were gone; many had skipped Sunday morning service to attend a series of spectacle entertainments. Looking out at the relatively sparse crowd, Augustine ascended the pulpit and said, "I am sure you remember the promise I made you . . . your graces will also remember that on Christmas morning I put off solving the question I had raised, because there were many people celebrating that day's feast [Christmas] with us, who usually find explanations of the word of God rather a bore. But now, I assume, it is only people who want to listen that have come together here."[64] He encouraged the faithful to pray for the their peers, because the spectacle entertainments "have blown many people away from here for whose salvation I am greatly concerned, and I urge you, brothers, to feel as much concern for them yourselves, and to pray earnestly to God for those who are not yet in earnest about the shows truth puts on, but are still given over to shows put on for the flesh."[65]

After praising those gathered for choosing to attend worship, Augustine preached that Christ was the greater and true spectacle of God. He contrasted the hunt in the stadium (*venationes*) with Christ, who "hunts into the nets of salvation" those who put on spectacle entertainments and the masses who populate the amphitheaters. He taught that the psalms prefigured Christ as a spectacle:

63. Salvian, *On the Government of God* 6.2.10, cited in Kyle, *Spectacles of Death in Ancient Rome*, 185. My italics.

64. Augustine, *Essential Sermons*, 64.

65. Ibid.

[Christ] told us himself, before he became a spectacle to be gaped at he foretold it himself, and in prophetic language he declared beforehand what was going to happen as if it already had. He said in the psalm, "They dug my hands and my feet, they counted all my bones" (Ps 22:16–17). There you have how he became a spectacle to be stared at, so that they even counted his bones. He goes on to call it a spectacle even more plainly: "They however, looked at me closely and stared at me" (Ps 22:17).[66]

Augustine also taught how Christ was depicted as a spectacle in the gospels, saying, "[Christ] was stared at in mockery, he was stared at by people who didn't even cheer him on in that show, but raged against him."[67] Finally, Augustine described how Paul in First Corinthians exhorted the church to follow Christ's example and become a spectacle. Just as God allowed Christ's body to be a spectacle, God has made the body of Christ, the church, to be a spectacle in the world: "In much the same way he had his witnesses and martyrs stared at in the beginning, as the apostle [Paul] says: 'We have become a spectacle to the world and to angels and to men' (1 Cor. 4:9)."[68]

Augustine's description of both the incarnate and ecclesial bodies of Christ as spectacle reflects his commitment to Paul's theology of the church. William Harmless observes that Augustine's "thinking admitted no sharp fissure between the real presence of Christ in the bread and the real presence of Christ within the community... [For Augustine] the Body of Christ appeared as a sort of diptych: at once people and as 'sanctified' bread."[69] Partaking of the Eucharist united members of the church with Christ and Christ with the church. Augustine contended that because Christians saw the spectacle of Christ's crucifixion differently than "the persecutor," the celebration of the Eucharist was not, as some pagans supposed, a reenactment of Christ's crucifixion. When Christians looked upon the crucifixion of Christ, or upon the death of a Christian martyr, they saw the spectacle in a different way: "Our interest in one and the same spectacle is quite different from that of the persecutor. He was enjoying the martyr's punishment, we its cause; he was taking pleasure in what he was suffering, we in why he was suffering; he in his torments, we in his strength ... because he

66. Ibid.
67. Ibid.
68. Ibid.
69. Harmless, *Augustine and the Catechumenate*, 319.

was abiding in the faith."[70] The Christian did not merely consume Christ through an objectifying gaze, but by bringing Christ close, took him into the body through eating and drinking. Consuming the Eucharist united the Christian with Christ's suffering and resurrection. Thus, Augustine taught that Eucharist necessarily involved a *conversion of seeing*. The Christian did not objectify Christ through a consuming gaze, but rather was someone who had been joined to his suffering and through it received an extraordinary gift.

Participating in the Eucharist also involved Christians in seeing the actual body and blood of Christ present in the elements of bread and wine. Augustine referred to this way of seeing as the *corpus mysticum Cristi*. In his catechetical sermons, Augustine taught newly baptized Christians, "What you can see here, dearly beloved, on the table of the Lord, is bread and wine; but this bread and wine, when the word is applied to it, becomes the body and blood of the Word."[71] Augustine insisted that learning to see this new reality required both theological instruction and *a conversion of desire*. Harmless observes, "The transformation of bread and wine into the Body and Blood of Christ did not preoccupy Augustine the way it would the medieval tradition. For Augustine, transformed bread and wine was but one half of the mystery: the other half, transformed people, was what especially concerned him."[72] In other words, for Augustine, the meaning of the metaphysical transformation of the Eucharist was grounded in the transformation of the baptized: "Augustine was convinced that faith was much more than theological know-how; it was rather a *habitus*, a whole web of attitudes, feelings, and behaviors that imbued and shaped the lives of the faithful."[73] Those seeking to participate in the Eucharist had to come to terms with the many forces that shaped their desires. Ultimately, for Augustine, the problem was not the flesh per se; the desires of the flesh exhibited a deeper problem: "The real culprit was the unruly human heart which clung to the wrong things or, more precisely, loved things in the wrong way."[74]

For Augustine, the body was the locus of a war between the demonic power of spectacle and the believer.[75] Early Christians "envisioned conversion

70. Augustine, *Essential Sermons*, 320.
71. Augustine, Sermon 229, in ibid., 283.
72. Harmless, *Augustine and the Catechumenate*, 318.
73. Ibid., 271.
74. Ibid., 255.
75. Ibid., 271.

in cosmological terms: it was marked by a metaphysical shift, a transfer of power from the reign of Satan to the reign of God. With this transfer of power came a change in status: the convert ceased to suffer Satan's tyranny and came to enjoy God's magnanimous rule."[76] Early Christians recognized "invisible demonic forces [that] wandered about wrecking havoc . . . [Satan's] influence seemed everywhere: it masqueraded under the guise of paganism and its accompanying apparatus (idols, sacrifices, amulets, astrology); his pomps were displayed in cultural institutions (the bloody public games, the theaters, the annual festivals); and his dark powers had seeped into every crevice of ordinary social life."[77] This did not mean that the demons and Satan were blamed for every sinful act of humankind. Augustine also taught that "the devil is not to be blamed for everything: there are times when a man may be his own devil."[78] However, before a person seeking membership in the church could partake of the Eucharist, he had to recognize how these demonic powers had come to possess him through his desires. Only then would he have the right spiritual appetite for consuming the Eucharist; only then could he see beyond the immediate appearance of bread and wine to the spiritual reality of body and blood. In *Confessions*, Augustine wrote that "bread, which is pleasant to a healthy palate, is repugnant to a sick one, and . . . diseased eyes hate the light which to the unclouded is delightful."[79]

Baptism and Exorcism

The catechumenate was the early church's chief weapon against the corrupting powers of spectacle and paganism. It was designed to reform the new Christian through an intense regimen of instruction, rigorous ascetic practice, and ritual exorcism. This regimen helped catechumens recognize how the Roman state and Greco-Roman culture, especially spectacle, had exercised power in their lives. John Chrysostom remarked, "the catechumen is a sheep without a seal; he is a deserted inn and a hostel without a door, which lies open to all without distinction; he is a lair for robbers, a refuge for wild beasts, a dwelling place for demons."[80] Catechesis

76. Ibid., 261.

77. Ibid.

78. Quoted in Harmless, *Augustine and the Catechumenate*, 272.

79. Augustine, *Confessions* 16.22 (Boulding, 176).

80. Chrysostom, *Baptismal Instruction* 10.16, in Harmless, *Augustine and the Catechumenate*, 59.

was designed to evacuate the unholy and unhealthy desires that held the catechumen captive. Ritual exorcism was an integral part of this process, because it signified the catechumen's inability to rid himself of these powers. He needed the power of Christ and the fellowship of other believers to achieve the seal of baptism and rebirth into the social order of the church.

In Augustine's time, the intense regimen deterred many catechumens from putting in their names for baptism. They remained nominal Christians and participated in worship services and catechetical instruction, but they never advanced to become full members of the church. This was common even for those raised in the church. For example, John Chrysostom remained unbaptized until the age of twenty-five, Basil of Caesarea was baptized at twenty-six, and Gregory of Nazianzus at twenty-eight. In *Confessions*, Augustine notes that like many parents, his mother, Monica, did not have him baptized as a child because she "knew how many great tides of temptation threatened me before I grew up, and she chose to let them beat upon the as yet unmolded clay rather than upon the finished image which had received the stamp of baptism."[81] Augustine understood from personal experience the rationale for refraining from baptism and full membership in the church.

Quodvultdeus of Carthage, a contemporary of Augustine, chided catechumens who preferred to remain nominally Christian rather than pursue baptism. He observed that many of them refrained from baptism because they wanted to continue to enjoy spectacle entertainment. He said, "You enter the church for a little to pour out prayers, yet in a short time you can be seen shouting shamelessly in the theatrical spectacles. What do the pomps of the devil, which you have renounced, mean to you? Why do you limp along as if you had a pair of swollen testicles? If God is your master, go after him; if the world, go after it."[82] Although his teaching was rather pointed, Quodvultdeus recognized the difficult situation of catechumens who struggled with their desires. They could not bring themselves to dive headlong into the baptismal waters because they were, like Augustine, torn between their old desires and the call of baptism. Augustine describes how, before his conversion, "A new will had begun to emerge in me, the will to worship disinterestedly and enjoy you, O God, our only sure felicity; but it was not yet capable of surmounting that earlier will strengthened by

81. Augustine, *Confessions*, 51–52.

82. Quodvultdeus, *Third Homily on the Creed* 1.14, in *Creedal Homilies*, 68.

inveterate custom. And so the two wills fought it out—the old and the new, one carnal, the other spiritual—and in their struggle tore my soul apart."[83] Quodvultdeus urged his students to "believe in such a way that you may desire to see what you believe."[84]

When a catechumen finally decided to "turn in his name" and move toward baptism, he or she would become a *competente*.[85] *Competentes* committed themselves to a Lenten program of ascetic practices, an intense regimen of instruction, and finally ritual exorcism. These practices tested their competency for membership in the church, and Augustine described this program as the "stages of curative treatment" (*ordo curationis*).[86] Harmless observes that this program of ascetic practice, instruction, and exorcism "was thoroughgoing enough that Augustine and his contemporaries thought of it more along the lines of a boot camp or fitness program than schooling. They presupposed—rightly or wrongly—that the *competentes* were the spiritually flabby, that they suffered from any of a host of addictions, and that these ailments had penetrated every fiber of their lives and could be healed only with a radical reshaping of habit that touched the whole person: physical, psychological, intellectual, social."[87]

Exorcism played a dramatic and important role in the process of conversion, and various metaphors were used to help new Christians understand its significance. For example, in the *Procatechesis*, Cyril of Jerusalem described exorcism as a refining fire: "Submit to the exorcisms devoutly . . . Imagine virgin gold alloyed with various foreign substances: copper, tin, iron, lead. What we are after is the gold alone."[88] Alternately, Theodore of Mopsuestia used a courtroom analogy: "By his words the exorcist showed that the candidate was innocent, that he had suffered a form of cruel slavery, and that the devil 'had forcibly and unjustly brought him under his rule.'"[89] Chrysostom used still another metaphor, describing the exorcists'

83. Augustine, *Confessions* 8.10 (Boulding, 192).

84. Quodvultdeus, *Third Homily on the Creed* 2.1, in *Creedal Homilies*, 69.

85. Finn, "It Happened One Saturday Night," 591.

86. Ibid., 595. Cf. Harmless, *Augustine and the Catechumenate*, 63.

87. Harmless, *Augustine and the Catechumenate*, 295.

88. Cyril of Jerusalem, *Procatechesis* 1, quoted in Harmless, *Augustine and the Catechumenate*, 68.

89. Theodore, *Catechetical Homily* 12.22–23, quoted in Harmless, *Augustine and the Catechumenate*, 68–69.

work to purify the *competentes* thus: "as if they were preparing a house for a royal visit, they cleanse your minds by those awesome words."[90]

In Augustine's North Africa, exorcism "evoked the familiar image of the slave auction, and Augustine and Quoduvultdeus repeatedly depicted them [*competentes*] as enslaved captives."[91] They stood before the congregation of the baptized, whose ranks they hoped to join, and the exorcist approached them as a representative of the church. Augustine described this process as the *sacramentum exorcismi*.[92] Alternately, Thomas Finn describes it as "ritual combat." Finn suggests, "The underlying principle in ritual is that two worlds intersect, the visible world of every day and the world of perception, conviction, and values that lies beyond the visible yet shapes and is shaped by it."[93] In exorcism "the two worlds which intersected . . . were the visible showdown between competent and exorcist on the one hand and the invisible showdown between the divine and diabolic on the other."[94] Since *competentes* were helpless, possessed by forces that ruled their desires, the exorcist and community of the baptized battled the enemy within them:

> The place of combat, the arena, was at once the church building and the church as community, signified by the encircling congregation. The subject of the drama was the competent, with the exorcist in the leading role. The stage directions and script were rites of the scrutiny. Very likely, however, competent and exorcist stood fact to face, more accurately bowed head to face. The hands of the exorcist were imposed, perhaps roughly, on the competent's shoulders, and the congregation as chorus chanted an interpretive psalm. In a stentorian voice and biblical language the exorcist assaulted the devil in the competent and sought to drive him out in the name of Christ, the Redeemer, and the Trinity. The contemptuous hissing of exsufflation brought the assault to a climax.[95]

When she had completed the ritual of exorcism, the competent renounced the empire before the whole congregation, saying, "I renounce the devil, his

---

90. Chrysostom, *Baptismal Instruction* 2.12. See Harmless, *Augustine and the Catechumenate*, 69.

91. Finn, "It Happened One Saturday Night," 603.

92. Ibid., 596.

93. Ibid.

94. Ibid.

95. Ibid., 602.

pomps, and his angels."[96] To reject the "pomps" of the devil was to reject the *pompa*, the religious processions that dramatically brought Rome's pagan gods into the spectacle entertainments. Finn observes that before the conversion of Constantine, the object of these words was the Roman state, and after it was the Greco-Roman world and its omnipresent culture. In one breath the *competentes* disowned both Satan and pagan culture, including spectacles and the worship of Caesar.

When the time came for the Easter Vigil, Augustine gathered the *competentes* to keep watch. During the night, they would recite the Creed before the assembled faithful,[97] and Augustine instructed them in the meaning of baptism, telling them that their old lives were passing away and they were being born anew. He said, "For we are buried together with Christ by baptism into death, that as he was raised from the dead so we also may walk in newness of life."[98] After receiving instruction, the candidates followed Augustine into the *consignatorium*, the small chapel that housed the baptismal font.[99] In Augustine's church, the font was rectangular and featured pillars at each of the four corners. Curtains may have hung between the pillars, and water likely jetted out and swirled in the font. This living water signified the new life into which the *competentes* were about to be born. Before entering the font, the *competentes* renounced Satan and swore allegiance to Christ. Finally, they stepped into the font to receive the seal of baptism and became neophytes or, as Augustine called them, *infantes*—infants in the faith. They received new white linen robes and sandals to signify their new birth and stainless new lives. Finally, the new *infantes* were invited to partake in Eucharist. They would, for the first time, consume the body of Christ and drink the blood of Christ. They experienced all of this without

96. See Quodvultdeus, *First Homily on the Creed* 1. 11, in *Creedal Homilies*, 24. Once evil had been renounced, the candidates were brought to the baptismal waters where they died to sin and were reborn in Christ. The community of the baptized embraced them, and they shared in their first Eucharist.

97. Augustine, *Sermon* 59.1. Cf. Harmless, *Augustine and the Catechumenate*, 306.

98. Augustine, Sermon 229. Cf. Harmless, *Augustine and the Catechumenate*, 306. Harmless notes that none of Augustine's actual baptismal catecheses have been preserved; however, his remarks in other sermons indicate what he said at the time of instruction. For example, in Sermon 229 Augustine is reminding the baptized of their baptismal experience and urging them to recall the significance of what they learned through catechesis.

99. I am indebted to William Harmless for the following description of the baptismal ritual in Augustine's church. See Harmless, *Augustine and the Catechumenate*, 307–8.

comment or instruction, and this silence was intentional. Experiencing the mystery of the *corpus mysticum Christi* was necessary before *infantes* could receive instruction.

Sacraments versus Paganism

When Easter morning broke, the church gathered in the basilica for worship, and in his Easter sermon, Augustine told the *infantes* that the great traditions they had experienced had finally "seized hold of them."[100] At the close of the Easter service, those catechumens who had not yet put in their names were dismissed. The baptized members of the church received the Eucharist, and at this point Augustine provided the *infantes* with instruction on the eucharistic mystery.[101]

With the *infantes* gathered closely around the wooden altar, he pointed to the fact that the elements of the Eucharist were ordinary: "What you see here, dearly beloved, on the table of the Lord, is bread and wine." The simplicity of the Christian sacraments contrasted sharply with the worship of paganism. Robin Lane Fox describes how pagan temples used elaborate apparatuses to provide worshipers with spectacular experiences of communing with divinities.[102] At Pompeii, new converts saw pagan gods by looking "through a glass darkly," and pagan priests utilized devices like temple doors that automatically swung open by unseen mechanisms to magically reveal the god or goddess. In Corinth, excavations of the temple of Dionysus unearthed an elaborate channel of underground piping that was used to turn water into wine. A practical textbook for pagan priests by Hero of Alexandria taught pagan priests how to engineer such mechanisms. This ancient technology provided special effects that made the gods present to the worshipers.

The Christian sacraments lacked the technology and spectacle that was involved in many pagan rituals. Tertullian noted that some people rejected Christian teaching on the contention that the simplicity of the sacraments was inconsistent with the grandeur of their effects. But Tertullian argued that the simplicity of the elements highlighted the true divine power

---

100. Augustine, Sermon, 228.3, Harmless, *Augustine and the Catechumenate*, 315.

101. Augustine's instruction on the Eucharist has been preserved in Sermons 227, 229, 229A, and 272.

102. Lane Fox, *Pagans and Christians*, 136–37.

behind them: "with so great simplicity, without pomp, without any considerable novelty of preparation, finally, without expense, a man is dipped in water and amid the utterance of some few words . . . the consequent attainment of eternity is esteemed the more incredible."[103] Similarly, Ambrose taught his skeptical catechumens, "You must not trust, then, wholly to your bodily eyes; that which is not seen is more really seen, for the object of sight is temporal, but that other eternal, which is not apprehended by the eye, but is discerned by the mind and spirit."[104]

Consuming as Binding

As Augustine continued his instruction, he helped the *infantes* recognize that the simple elements of the eucharistic mystery were also food. He urged them to "call to mind what this created object was, not so long ago, in the fields; how the earth produced it, the rain nourished it, ripened it into the full ear; then human labor carried it to the threshing floor, threshed it, winnowed it, stored it, brought it out, ground it, mixed it into dough, baked it . . . and produced it finally as bread."[105] Augustine then likened the process of making bread to the catechumenate, teaching the *infantes* that when they were catechumens they were "stored in the barn," but when they gave in their names and became *competentes* they "began to be ground [as grain] by fasts and exorcisms."[106] With the waters of baptism they were "moistened into dough and made into one lump."[107] Finally, with the flame of the Holy Spirit they were "baked and made into the Lord's loaf of bread."[108] Augustine also described the *infantes* as the cup of the Sacrament: "And you, after those fasts, after those hard labors, after the humiliation and contrition, have now at last come, in the name of Christ *into* the Lord's cup, so to say; and there you are on the table, and there you are in the cup."[109] When the *infantes* responded, he told them, "*It is to what you yourselves are that you reply amen.*"[110]

103. Tertullian, "On Baptism," 669.
104. Ambrose, *On Mysteries*, New Advent online.
105. Augustine, *Essential Sermons*, 283
106. Ibid.
107. Ibid.
108. Ibid.
109. Ibid., 284.
110. Ibid.

Through consuming the body and blood of Christ, the *infantes* had become bound to one another and to the society of the church. Augustine said, "This bread is a sign of unity. So too the wine was there in many grapes, and has now been concentrated into a unity." Consuming the Eucharist initiated the *infantes* into an alternative community based on a different form of desire and a different way of seeing the world. In Christ they had a new life. Of course, Augustine knew that this marked the beginning of their faith as full Christian believers. Some of them would struggle in the coming months and even years to have their desires fully transformed. The allure of spectacle might tempt some back into the Coliseum or amphitheaters of the empire. He knew that even his own conversion was a process of learning to see and desire the eucharistic feast of God. In *Confessions*, he wrote, "Then did I perceive your invisible reality through created things, but to keep my gaze there was beyond my strength. I was forced back through weakness and returned to my familiar surroundings, bearing with me only a loving memory, one that yearned for something of which I had caught the fragrance, but could not yet feast upon."[111] Nevertheless, Augustine had confidence that even if the *infantes* returned to consumption of the spectacles, where the blood of the sacrificial victim was not the blood of Christ, they had taken Christ into themselves and been united with the church. Ultimately, God's grace would continue to work in their lives, calling them back from the empty consumption of the spectacles to the life-giving and satisfying feast of the church.

Augustine on Spectacle and Demonic Ontology

In *City of God*, Augustine directly charged Roman politicians with corrupting Roman society with spectacle entertainments, which he regarded as the worship of demons. He said, "Demons can only get control of men when they have deluded and deceived them; in the same way the leaders of men (who were not men of integrity, but the human counterparts of the demons) taught men as true, under the name of religion, things they knew to be false . . . .What chance had a weak and ignorant individual of escaping from the *combined deceits of the statesmen and the demons*?"[112]

111. Augustine, *Confessions*, 177–78.

112. Augustine, *City of God* 4.32 (Bettenson, 176). My italics. In *Confessions* Augustine observed that the children of Rome's ruling elite were caught in a vicious cycle: "The people who provide these [spectacle] entertainments enjoy such celebrity and public

Like other early Christians leaders before him, Augustine regarded spectacle as a particularly powerful manifestation of demonic power: "For such demons are pleased . . . with the frenzy of the games, with the cruelty of the amphitheater, with the violent contests of those who undertake strife and controversy . . . By acting in this way [pagans] offer incense to the demons within their hearts. For the deceptive spirits rejoice in seduction; they feast upon the evil customs and the notoriously vile life of those whom they have misled and entrapped."[113]

Before moving to the next chapter, where we will bring Augustine's understanding of the Eucharist as an alternative to spectacle and consumption, we must further explore the relationship between spectacle and Augustine's understanding of demons. Many pagans would not have found the charge of demon worship strange or necessarily damning. Demon worship was relatively common and acceptable in Roman paganism, and it played an integral role in spectacle entertainments. For example, lead "curse tablets" (*tabellae difixionis*) found in the amphitheater at Carthage in North Africa contain prayers of solicitation to gods and demons against opponents in a spectacle entertainment; one such tablet read, "I conjure you up, prematurely dead demon . . . by the powerful names of Salbal . . . Paralyze them in their course, destroy their power, their soul and speed."[114]

Since demon worship was acceptable to many Romans, Augustine took up the challenge of explaining why it was erroneous and contradictory. He observed that the Roman propensity for demon worship was part of a Neoplatonic ontology that conceived of communion with divinity as a matter of overcoming the limits of human embodiment and mortality. Romans regarded demons as mediators between the wretched situation of mortal human beings and the immortal existence of the gods. Augustine noted that for pagans there is "a threefold division of all beings possessed of a rational soul; there are gods, men and demons. The gods occupy the most exalted situation; mankind has the most lowly; and the demons are in

---

esteem that nearly all of them hope their children will follow their example; and yet they are quite prepared to see those children beaten for watching similar shows to the detriment of their study, study which, as their parents hope, will bring them to a position in which they in turn will provide the shows!" (1.10, 16; Boulding, 13–14).

113. Augustine, *Sermons* 198.3.

114. Cited in Thomas Finn's introduction to Quodvultdeus, *Creedal Homilies*, 16. For more on Carthaginian curse tablets, see Bomgardner, *Story of the Roman Amphitheatre*, 138.

between."[115] As beings situated between embodied immanence and absolute transcendence, the demons are immortal, but like human beings they suffer from the afflictions or passions of the soul, including lust, greed, and gluttony. Since demons are subject to the passions of the soul, "it is not remarkable, the Platonists tell us, that they delight in the obscenities of the shows [e.g., spectacle entertainments] and the fantasies of the poets, seeing that they are subject to human desires, which are remote from the gods, and altogether alien to them."[116] Although pagans regarded demons as not fully divine, they esteemed them as worthy of worship.

Augustine objected to the notion that demons could serve as mediators by virtue of their immortal bodies: "as if religion, by which men aspire to be united with the gods by the mediation of demons, were located in the body."[117] He insisted that a deity worthy of worship would never enjoy the bloodlust and violence of Rome's spectacle entertainments. Moreover, Augustine observed that not just demons but the gods themselves were honored by the obscenities of spectacle entertainments. He pointedly asked his pagan interlocutors, "who are the gods who like the stage shows and demand that those spectacles should be included in the divine ceremonies and exhibited among the honors paid to them?"[118] Augustine insisted that on the basis of their own Neoplatonic ontology, pagans had to admit that their deities were not truly gods but mere demons who were subject to the passions of the soul as evinced by their enjoyment of spectacle entertainments. Thus, Augustine claimed that people who worship pagan gods merely commune with demons rather than true divinity, for "the mind of the demons is in subjection to the passions of desire, of fear, of anger, and the rest."[119]

Augustine argued that the real problem separating human beings from God was not merely mortality and embodiment but perverted and misguided desire: "our need is not for a mediator with an immortal body, like the bodies on high, but with a diseased soul . . . [Rather,] we need a mediator linked with us in our lowliness by reason of the mortal nature of his body, and yet able to render us truly divine assistance for our purification

115. Augustine, *City of God* 8.14 (Bettenson, 318).
116. Ibid.
117. Ibid., 9.9 (Bettenson, 354).
118. Ibid., 8.8 (Bettenson, 317).
119. Ibid., 9.6 (Bettenson, 350).

and liberation, through the immortal justice of his spirit in virtue of which he has remained in his dwelling on high."[120] Augustine contended that this mediator was Jesus Christ, the Incarnate One, who alone had united humanity and divinity in his body: "Demons are not to be reckoned our superiors because they are not creatures of flesh. This mediator is, as the holy Scripture proclaims, 'the mediator between God and mankind, the man Christ Jesus (1 Tim 2:5). In respect of his divinity, he is always equal to the Father, and by his humanity he became like us."[121] Christ not only mediated between embodied humanity and divine Spirit, he provided a way for humanity to reconfigure their passions of the soul, thereby obtaining the goodness of God: "[W]e direct our course toward him with love (*dilectio*), so that in reaching him we may find our rest, and attain our happiness because we have achieved our fulfillment in him. For our Good, that Final Good about which the philosophers dispute, is nothing else but to cleave to him."[122]

Augustine claimed that when mortal humans cleaved to Jesus Christ, they were in a more favorable position than demons who possessed immortal bodies. He observed that Plotinus, who "is accorded the praise of having understood Plato more thoroughly than anyone else, at any rate in modern times," shared this same perspective: "That is, [Plotinus] considered that the very fact of man's corporal mortality is due to the compassion of God, who would not have us kept forever in the misery of this life. The wickedness of the demons was not judged worthy of this compassion, and in the misery of their condition, with a soul subject to passions, they have not been granted the mortal body, which man has received, but an eternal body."[123] Thus mortality is not, as the pagans contended, a liability, but rather a gift from God, because mortality forces humans to look to God for the conversion of their desires (cf. Gen 3:22). Demons, on the other hand, engaged in wicked desire without consequence, because of their immortal-

120. Ibid., 9.17 (Bettenson, 364).

121. In *City of God* Augustine writes, "As man he is our Mediator; as man he is our way. For there is hope to attain a journey's end when there is a path which stretches between the traveller and his goal. But if there is no path, or if a man does not know which way to go, there is little use in knowing the destination. As it is, there is one road, and one only, well secured against all possibility of going astray; and this road is provided by one who is himself both God and man. As God, he is the goal; as man, he is the way" (11.2 [Bettenson, 431]).

122. Ibid., 10.3 (Bettenson, 376).

123. Ibid., 9.10 (Bettenson, 355).

ity. Augustine described their existence as "topsy-turvy" because they were condemned to an existence of eternal, insatiable desire: "These demons . . . have been tied up and suspended as it were topsy-turvy, with their body, the servant, in the company of the blessed gods, and their soul, the master, in the company of wretched men; exalted in the lower part of their being, they are abased in their upper part."[124]

The Coliseum simulated the topsy-turvy existence of the demons by elevating the spectators above the death and suffering occuring on the amphitheater floor. From his privileged seat, the spectator looked down upon the mortality of the victims as if he were gazing it all as an immortal demon. Through an objectifying gaze, he consumed the excitement and psychosexual allure of the spectacular violence. The unfolding drama of death ignited his lusts and most wicked desires; such desires were enflamed when a lion ripped a man's arm from his body or when a gladiator delivered the deathblow. By means of a consuming gaze, he experienced life as a topsy-turvy demon, immortal yet rapt in the passions of the soul.

Summary

This chapter has provided a description of Jesus' crucifixion and of the Eucharist in light of the role spectacle played in the politics of the Roman Empire. In addition, it has briefly described the relationship between spectacle and Augustine's demonic ontology. Before moving to chapter 2, in which we will bring these themes to bear on the modern experience of spectacle, it is helpful to characterize early Christianity as an alternative to Rome's society of the spectacle:

---

124. Ibid., 9.9 (Bettenson, 354).

Rome's Society of the Spectacle	The Early Church
1. Roman politicians such as Pontius Pilate were greatly influenced by the appetites of the people they governed. Spectacle entertainments distracted the populace from other concerns and frustrations and placed the sponsor in a favorable light. However, the people's appetite for spectacle could undermine the authority of a Roman ruler, and Pilate's concern for justice was eclipsed by the crowd's desire to consume Jesus' body and blood as spectacle.	1. Jesus willingly became a spectacle in order to "draw men unto me," and the Eucharist reconceives what it means to consume the body and blood of Jesus. It redirects this desire toward the gift of Christ, who truly satisfies human desire. Augustine, Quodvultdeus, and other early theologians taught that those seeking to become Christians had to rid themselves of the desire to consume spectacle in order to taste of the true spectacle, namely, Jesus.
2. Spectacle is a perverse Eucharist in which the body and blood of the victim are objects that are consumed through gazing (as when Alypius "drank in" the blood of spectacle in Augustine's *Confessions*).	2. Augustine taught that by partaking in the Eucharist, Christians learn to gaze Jesus' crucifixion differently and to see the spiritual reality present in the bread and wine. The Christian understands Jesus' body and blood not as objects for consumption but as means of participation in his death and resurrection.
3. Paganism worships demons as intermediaries between humanity and divinity. Demons are *neither* human *nor* divine but exist between divinity and humanity. Like gods, they are immortal, but like human beings, they are subject to the passions of the soul.	3. Augustine taught that Christ, not demons, is the true mediator between humanity and God. Christ is *both* human *and* divine. In his sacrifice he gave eternal life to humanity and freed them from the passions of the soul.

3

Modern Spectacle, Politics, and the Fellowship of the Demons

The past is never dead. It's not even the past.

—WILLIAM FAULKNER

Politics, Spectacle, and the Meta-Arena

This chapter investigates connections between ancient Roman culture and the modern society of the spectacle in order to learn what early Christianity can teach us about being the church today. The last chapter described ways spectacle played a powerful role in Roman politics and government. Today, spectacle plays a role in modern American politics and government. This commonality is not coincidental. In 2010, the United States National Constitution Center in Philadelphia featured an exhibit titled "Ancient Rome and America." The exhibit was designed to help U.S. citizens "discover the many ways in which Americans have imagined ourselves to be a nation built in the image of ancient Rome."[1] For example, patrons to the exhibit were told, "Before it was an empire, Rome was a city ruled by a king. Americans followed in Rome's footsteps over two thousand years later when they overthrew a British king and founded a republic of their own. Americans often invoked the memory of the heroes and legends of ancient Rome. In this way the ideals and virtues of republican Rome became a part of the

1. National Constitution Center, "Ancient Rome and America: Exhibition Overview," http://constitutioncenter.org/media/files/rome_exhibition.pdf, 1. "Ancient Rome and America" was on display from February 19 to August 1, 2010.

61

foundation of America."[2] One of the key similarities between Rome and America is voting in political elections. Beacham observes that republican Rome displayed "significant democratic features" in that the voice of the people was central to the political process. Roman politics involved "the necessity of winning elections to attain office, and often victory depended on securing decisive support not just from the upper strata but from the general urban population of Rome. Particularly toward the end of the Republic, the role of popular political expression in determining fundamental questions of citizens' rights, the conduct of foreign and military affairs, and the exercise of leadership was crucial."[3]

The fathers of American democracy fashioned their new country after the Roman Republic, but in so doing they failed to realize that a politics of the people has a dark side: the *vox ominum*, the roar of the arena spectators. Peter Sloterdijk has observed that today democracy has returned to the sociology of the Roman Coliseum and of spectacle entertainment, and he notes that "sufficient account has yet to be given of the fact that the strongest symbol and media of ancient mass culture—I am speaking of the Roman arena—actually only made a comeback in the twentieth century . . . We had to wait until the twentieth century for this socio-architectural idea of space and of gathering to experience a revival; and when it did, it was in epidemic dimensions."[4] Today's modern media has replaced the Roman arena as the public space where spectacle and politics converge. Whereas Roman politicians accumulated political power by investing enormous sums of money in the spectacle entertainments, modern politicians invest millions of dollars in the spectacles of the modern media's meta-arena. As

2. Ibid., 2.

3. Beacham, *Spectacle Entertainments of Early Imperial Rome*, 3–4.

4. Sloterdijk, *Neither Sun Nor Death*, 120. Sloterdijk observes that the return of the arena is both architectural and dramaturgical. On the one hand, American culture has recovered the architecture and spectacle entertainments of the Roman arena. For example, the Super Bowl is remarkably similar to Roman gladiatorial competition. As did Roman gladiatorial spectacles, the Super Bowl features men "fighting" one another on the floor of a great stadium, and as did Roman spectacle, the Super Bowl incorporates ritual feasting (Super Bowl parties) and dramatic displays of patriotism (e.g., singing the national anthem). Rome utilized spectacle to tell its people the story of its great history and achievements in war. Similarly, the 2011 Super Bowl featured a six-minute presentation telling the story of the Declaration of Independence, which included its full recitation. On the other hand, the significance of the return of the Roman arena in contemporary Western culture is not limited to the spheres of architecture and sports but extends to every aspect of social life, especially politics.

Michael Hardt and Antonio Negri observe, "the law of the spectacle clearly reigns in the realm of media-driven electoral politics."[5]

In some ways, American democracy has actually surpassed Rome in uniting spectacle and politics. To illustrates this, let us compare the campaigns of the 2008 presidential election in the United States with the political strategy of the Roman Emperor Commodus. By all accounts Commodus was a ruthless and narcissistic dictator who, in the third century, wanted to enhance his public and political image by portraying himself as Gladiator of gladiators. Although gladiators were condemned criminals, some achieved great fame and status as celebrities, and Commodus believed that by displaying himself as a gladiatorial champion, he would gain this renown himself. However, his attempt at celebrity elicited harsh criticism from the Roman people, because he had "entered the arena personally and polluted himself by acting as a gladiator . . . [H]e was an embarrassment to the elite and a threatening tyrant to the masses."[6] Like modern celebrities, Roman gladiators represented a paradox. On the one hand, they were revered for exhibiting ideals such as strength and courage, but on the other hand they were reviled as social degradations. Thus, the notion of a celebrity emperor appalled the Roman people, and they viewed Commodus as having transgressed social mores. The Roman people dubbed him "the gladiator" and eventually killed him as an enemy of the state.[7] In the minds of the Roman people, providing spectacle entertainments was the duty of politicians, but politicians were *never* to enter the arena and become the spectacle itself.

The notion of a celebrity emperor may have appalled the Roman people, but in American democracy politics and celebrity go hand in hand. For example, during the presidential election of 2008, the Republican candidate, John McCain, was down in the polls and struggling to compete with his Democratic opponent, Barack Obama. In an attempt to defame Obama, McCain's campaign team launched a new strategy designed to portray him as a celebrity. The McCain team assumed that the American people would turn away from a celebrity president, but as it turned out, voters did not mind. Although he did not wholeheartedly embrace the celebrity label, Obama did not refuse it either. He and his political team keenly discerned that celebrity and spectacle are integral to the electoral process. As

---

5. Hardt and Negri, *Empire*, 322.

6. Kyle, *Spectacles of Death in Ancient Rome*, 225. For a discussion of Commodus as a celebrity gladiator, see ibid., 224–28.

7. Ibid., 225.

John Heilemann and Mark Halperin explain, "More than any election in memory, 2008 was a battle in which the candidates were celebrities, larger-than-life characters who crashed together to create a story uncommonly emotional for politics; a drama rich and captivating . . . *a multimedia spectacle* that unspooled 24/7 on the Web, cable television, the late-night talk shows, and *Saturday Night Live*. The drama played out against a backdrop that was itself vividly cinematic."[8] Similarly, Hardt and Negri observe, "The notion that politicians function as celebrities and that political campaigns operate on the logic of advertising are today taken for granted. Political discourse is an articulated sales pitch, and political participation is reduced to selecting among consumable images."[9]

Today, politicians must *take to the floor* of the media's meta-arena, engaging in its spectacle entertainments, including talk shows, comedy shows, and the twenty-four-hour news cycle. As Ross McKibbin notes, the typical politician is "'good at politics'—which means being good at *the mechanics* of politics, not necessarily at its ideas. The consequence is that the mechanics drives out the ideas, and the immediate expels the long-term . . . The crucial relationship now is between the politician, the journalist and the [political] 'adviser.'"[10] Moreover, political campaigns, says Ken Surin, are "almost exclusively media-focused and driven by the systemically induced compulsion to garner votes for the sake of being at the top of the electoral count no matter what."[11]

The meta-arena has played an important role in American politics for many years. Recalling the presidency of Bill Clinton and the Monica Lewinsky scandal of the 1990s, Sloterdijk observes that Clinton successfully navigated the spectacle of political scandal as if he were a skilled fighter in Rome's Coliseum: "If Clinton emerged more or less intact from the affair, it is only because he actually accepted the circus rules and held good right to the end, like an experienced gladiator."[12] As the 2012 U.S. presidential election approached, politicians seemed even more aware of their status as performers in a meta-arena who must please the crowd in order to win political office.

---

8. Heilemann and Halperin, *Game Change*, 9. My italics.

9. Hardt and Negri, *Empire*, 322.

10. Quoted in Surin, *Freedom Not Yet*, 11. My italics.

11. Ibid., 10.

12. Sloterdijk, *Neither Sun Nor Death*, 125.

The convergence of spectacle and politics raises serious questions about the viability of liberal democracy, and this is reflected in the thought of many philosophers and political theorists. For example, in *Democracy in What State?* a cohort of leading scholars, including Alain Badiou, Slavoj Žižek, Giorgio Agamben, Jean-Luc Nancy, Wendy Brown, Jacques Ranciere, Kristin Ross, and Daniel Ben, discuss the problems facing liberal democracy and its weakness as a political system. Badiou remembers that "for Plato, the trajectory that begins with the delights of democracy ends with the nightmare of tyranny," because once the demos begins to value its freedoms above all else, there is no avoiding the fundamental "link between democracy and nihilism."[13] Like Badiou, Brown argues that the uncritical embrace of modern notions of freedom is both naïve and historically unfounded. She asks,

> what historical evidence or philosophical precept permits us to assert that human beings want, as Dostoevsky had it, "freedom rather than bread"? All the indications of the past century are that, between the seductions of the market, the norms of disciplinary power, and the insecurities generated by an increasingly unbounded and disorderly human geography, the majority of Westerners have come to prefer moralizing, consuming, conforming, luxuriating, fighting, simply being told what to be, think, and do over the task of authoring their own lives . . . And if humans do not want the responsibility of freedom, and are neither educated nor encouraged in the project of political freedom, what does this mean for political arrangements that assume this desire and orientation?[14]

There has always been a link between the freedoms of modern democracy and economic prosperity, and democracy has been an indispensible means of liberating peoples around the world from tyrannical rule. On the other hand, America's Founding Fathers never anticipated that the foremost concern of a free citizenry would become the status of the market economy; they never intended for democratic freedoms to be synonymous with the proliferation of consumer culture. D. Stephen Long observes that our contemporary notions of freedom are grounded in modern liberalism, which "assumes we can determine the conditions for our knowledge of the good a priori, that is, that we can know the conditions for the possibility of good

13. Badiou, "Democratic Emblem," 13.

14. Brown, "We Are All Democrats Now . . ." 54–55.

without actually knowing the good. It calls those conditions *freedom*."¹⁵ In other words, modernity conceives freedom as the transvaluation of all other forms of the good. This notion of freedom leads us to believe that living the good life does not mean embodying goodness, truth, and beauty, but being free to do as I please. When this notion of freedom is combined with consumer culture, freedom comes to mean unqualified liberation of desire and acquisition of material possessions. To the extent that we adopt this notion of freedom, we repeat the mistakes of Rome's society of consumption and excess. Augustine's *City of God* was written more than fifteen hundred years ago, but his sardonic critique of Roman culture echoes across the centuries; it is as if he were speaking of America's "freedom-loving" consumer society:

> They are unconcerned about the utter corruption of their country. "So long as it lasts," they say, "so long as it enjoys material prosperity . . .What concerns us is that we should get richer all the time, to have enough for extravagant spending every day . . . Anyone who disapproves of this kind of happiness should rank as a public enemy: anyone who attempts to change it or get rid of it should be hustled out of hearing by the *freedom-loving* majority: he should be kicked out, and removed from the land of the living. We should reckon the true gods to be those who see that the people get this happiness."¹⁶

Modern democracy has undergone a significant shift. The rational Citizen Subject, who in the eighteenth and nineteenth centuries was posited as the bedrock of democratic freedom, has become the *Consuming Subject* of a new social and political order: the society of the spectacle.¹⁷ As Ken

---

15. Long, *Goodness of God*, 123.

16. Augustine, *City of God* 2.20 (Bettenson, 71). My italics.

17. I will say more below about the shift from the Citizen Subject of modern democracy to the Consumer Subject of the society of the spectacle. Building on the work of Etienne Balibar, Ken Surin provides a very helpful description of the Citizen Subject, including its basis in the transcendental metaphysics of Kantian philosophy (see Surin, *Freedom Not Yet*, 21–33). He argues that the decline of the Citizen Subject coincides with the demise of transcendental metaphysics. I will argue that the decline of the Citizen Subject resulted in a metaphysical void that has been filled by the demonic metaphysics of the society of the spectacle. Demonic metaphysics, which Augustine understood as the space between embodiment and immortality and between the human passions of the soul and divine immutability, is the ontological foundation of the Consumer Subject. Its prevalence in consumer culture signals a postsecular return to pagan religiosity and idolatry, the alternative to which is the theological metaphysics of Christian worship as expressed in the Eucharist. Whereas consumption in the society of the spectacle is a participation in a demonic transcendence (which is a mere approximation of communion

Surin observes, "In place of the Citizen Subject posited as an ideal by the liberal-democratic political systems of the past two centuries by and large now stands a new kind of ideal subject, to wit, a consumer subject cajoled and tutored in this country by Disney, Fox News, and *USA Today*."[18] Surin further observes that the degradation of the Citizen Subject of modern democracy "dovetailed with the wholesale incorporation of electoral politics into the society of the spectacle."[19] As a result of the convergence of politics and spectacle, the electoral process becomes

> the mere business of manipulating and dragooning voters according to the largely fictitious rhythms of election cycles. In this "postpolitical" politics (not to be conflated with the "apolitical" annihilation of anything to do with politics), politicians and their attendant logos and slogans are advertised and marketed to their somewhat bemused and docile constituencies like the hard-to-differentiate fizzy beverages typically found in American and European vending machines. Politicians in America and Britain today have to possess a "brand" in order to succeed; hence in the 2008 U.S. presidential election, the McCain "Maverick" brand apparently flopped with the electorate, while Obama's "Mr. Cool" brand was deemed to have been a success.[20]

The predictability of the Consumer Subject's response to the branding and marketing of political candidates corresponds with an astounding ignorance of the basic elements of the political process and democratic government. A 2007 study by the Annenberg Foundation revealed that only one-third of Americans could name the three branches of government.[21] The same study revealed that only 15 percent of Americans could name the Chief Justice of the Supreme Court, but 66 percent of Americans could name the judges on *American Idol*.[22] Consumer Subjects have abandoned

---

with Divine Transcendence), the Eucharist is an alternative "consumption" of the body and blood of Christ that facilitates a true participation in God. When we see Consumer Subjectivity in the light of the Eucharist, we realize that it is misdirected longing for God that is redeemed by being re-membered to the body of Christ.

18. Surin, *Freedom Not Yet*, 31.

19. Ibid., 9.

20. Ibid., 10.

21. Ibid.

22. Annenberg Center for Public Policy, "Partisan Judicial Elections Foster Cynicism and Distrust." Similarly, Ken Surin observes that in the 2004 and 2008 U.S. presidential elections "the 'low-information voter' who knows almost nothing of a political platform or prospectus, but who can be relied on to be enticed by the media-conveyed 'brand' of

the eighteenth-century ethos of the rational Citizen Subject as articulated by the founding fathers of modern democracy, but they are quite enthralled by spectacle. It would seem that history has repeated itself. What Juvenal said of the sovereignty and self-rule of the Roman people applies to today's modern democracy: "The Roman people which once dispensed power, consulships, legions, everything, now sits on its hands and anxiously waits for just two things: bread and games [spectacles]."[23]

Although the Consumer Subjects of the modern society of the spectacle have exchanged their sovereignty for bread and spectacle, they are neither passive nor docile. Even virtuous and well-meaning politicians cower before the collective roar of Consumer Subjects. Their noble political ideals quickly melt before the media's twenty-four-hour news cycle, which incessantly appeals to Consumer Subjects with political scandal and spectacle instead of genuine analysis of complex political issues. Ann Wroe's description of Roman politics in the era of Pontius Pilate is an apt illustration of the challenges modern politicians face: "With a small group of men you could talk rationally; but the crowd had to be harangued at maximum volume, with sweeping gestures, and in the process all subtlety of thought would disappear . . . Only the most primitive of ideas could get through; ideas requiring a yes or no. You roared into the answering roar."[24] The roar of the crowd overwhelms today's politicians as it did Pontius Pilate. And like Pilate our politicians are less concerned with truth and justice than with placating the *vox ominum* in order to guarantee their political ascendency and survival.

The displacement of the Citizen Subject by the Consumer Subject also means that the state of the economy dominates genuine political discourse. Consumer Subjects regard political officials as responsible for providing jobs so that they can participate in the means of production and consumption. It is not enough to have basic "human rights" as conceived in the eighteenth century with the signing of the Declaration of Independence. Nor is it enough to have the economic means to support one's self and family. For the Consumer Subject, anything short of the opulent American Dream signifies an unfulfilled life. The society of the spectacle constructs personhood

---

this or that politician with an appealing 'personality' . . . became crucial for the pollsters, focus groups, and public relations consultants of the major political parties" (*Freedom Not Yet*, 10).

23. Juvenal, *Satires* 10.72–81, cited in Mahoney, *Roman Sports and Spectacles*, 86.

24. Wroe, *Pontius Pilate*, 249.

around the ability to consummate the desires it incessantly cultivates in each individual. Without the consummation of consumer desire, the Consumer Subject feels like a second-class citizen. Experiencing the desire to consume and acting on that desire is how the Consumer Subject experiences the meaning of life as constructed by the society of the spectacle's symbolic order. Marketing plays an essential role in the generation of this symbolic order and in the cultivation of consumer desire. Debord observed that this intentional cultivation of desire alienates consumers from themselves: "The more he contemplates, the less he lives . . . [and] the less he understands his own life and his own desires . . . The individual gestures are no longer his own; they are the gestures of someone else who represents them to him."[25] As Steve Jobs of Apple Computer once famously said, "People don't know what they want until you show it to them."[26]

Badiou notes that Plato regarded democracy as unsustainable because democracy inevitably subjects the people to "the overt circulation of desires, of the objects on which these desires fix, and of the cheap thrills they deliver, and it's within this circulation that the subject is constituted."[27] To illustrate the relevance of Plato's insights for today, Badiou translates Plato's *Republic* into contemporary idiom. Plato's description of the democratic man (*homo democratus*) as rendered by Badiou is the quintessential Consumer Subject of the society of the spectacle:

> Democratic man lives only for the pure present, transient desire is his only law. Today he regales himself with a four-course dinner and vintage wine, tomorrow he is all about Buddha, ascetic fasting, streams of crystal clear water, and sustainable development. Monday he tries to get back in shape by pedaling for hours on a stationary bicycle; Tuesday he sleeps all day, then smokes and gorges again in the evening. Wednesday he declares that he is going to read some philosophy, but prefers doing nothing in the end. At Thursday's dinner party he crackles with zeal for politics, fumes indignantly at the next person's opinion, and heatedly denounces the society of consumption and spectacle. That evening he goes to see a Ridley Scott blockbuster about medieval warriors. Back home, he falls to sleep and dreams of liberating oppressed peoples by force of arms. Next morning he goes to work, feeling distinctly seedy, and tries without success to seduce the secretary from the office next door. He's been turning things over and has made up

25. Debord, *Society of the Spectacle*, 16
26. Sager and Burrows, "Back to the Future at Apple."
27. Badiou, "Democratic Emblem," 11.

his mind to get into real estate and go for the big money. But now
the weekend has arrived, and this economic crisis isn't going away,
so next week will be soon enough for all that. There you have a life,
or lifestyle, or lifeworld, or whatever you want to call it: no order,
no ideas, but nothing too disagreeable or distressing either. It is as
free as it is unsignifying, and insignificance isn't too high a price
to pay for freedom.[28]

It certainly seems that Plato's insights about democracy as recounted
by Badiou have proven to be true. History is a great teacher, and to the
extent that modern democracy has become the society of the spectacle, it
is following in the footsteps of its Roman predecessor. So what are we to do
with this realization and with the problem of Consumer Subjectivity? And
what is the church's role? No one is immune from the effects of the consumer society on our desires and longings. We may want different things
and in different ways, but if we are honest we must admit that we are, to a
greater or lesser extent, Consumer Subjects.

To address this issue of Consumer Subjectivity and the society of
the spectacle, the remaining pages of this chapter consider the Consumer
Subject as full of religious longing, which he seeks to fulfill through consumption. From this perspective, modern marketing can be understood
as the pagan liturgy of the modern society of the spectacle. Marketers are
especially adept at manipulating the subject through the use of images.
Whereas Roman paganism used images and idols to facilitate the worship
of its many gods, the modern society of the spectacle utilizes the power
of images as a mechanism for cultivating religious longing in the subject
in order to form him as a consumer. Guy Debord described the modern
society of the spectacle as the worship of a "factitious God" and observed
that spectacle is full of "metaphysical subtleties." However, he failed to identify or describe the nature of this metaphysics. For him it was enough to
equate the society of the spectacle with religion and condemn them both.
Today's contemporary Marxist theorists, like Hardt and Negri, maintain
this perspective. However, through a nuanced theological analysis we will
differentiate Christian metaphysics from the neo-pagan metaphysics of the
society of the spectacle by understanding the latter as a demonic ontology: an idealizing of immortality and the passions of the soul. Demonic
ontology is visible everywhere in the images that pervade the society of

28. This is Alain Badiou's "hyper-translation" of Plato's *The Republic*, 8.561d. Badiou
says that the aim of this translation "is to show that Plato is one of our foremost contemporaries" ("Democratic Emblem," 13).

the spectacle. These images are the idols and liturgy of the society of the spectacle's pagan religiosity. They correspond to a spiritual malformation for which the antidote is an analogical participation in God made possible by the Eucharist. In the gift of the Eucharist, Christ invites the Consumer Subject to turn his insatiable desire and limitless consumption toward the metaphysics of the Eucharist. The recipient of the Eucharist ceases to be a Consumer Subject because the "True Spectacle" has redeemed his desires, and through this redemption he has become part of a new political subjectivity. To paraphrase a famous line of Augustine's *Confessions*, you made us for yourself, O Lord. And our hearts are restless until they find their rest, *not in the demonic ideal of insatiable desire and limitless consumption*, but in you.

Origins of the Consumer Subject and Demonic Metaphysics

In order to understand the Consumer Subject, we have to trace its origins in the political subjectivity that emerged in modernity. Following Etienne Balibar, Ken Surin describes how the modern political subject, whom he describes as the Citizen Subject, emerged from the transcendental philosophy of Immanuel Kant. Kant sought to free individuals from the "self-inflicted tutelage that arises when we can't make judgments without the supervision of the other; this of course includes the tutelage of the king."[29] Kant accomplished this freedom by breaking with the ontological tradition of "his scholastic precursors when he declined to view Being [God] as the transcendental of the transcendentals, and instead made truth and judgment function in place of Being in his first *Critique*."[30] This new ontology moved beyond the Cartesian *subjectus* (who was still a subject of God) and made him subject only to Reason. Surin suggests, "Kant's great achievement lay in his simultaneous creation of the transcendental subject (i.e., the *subjectum* of modern epistemology) and the philosophical discrediting of the *subjectus* of the previous theologico-philosophical and political dispensation."[31]

For Kant, Reason exists as a self-grounding, transcendental Absolute, which is external to the subject himself.[32] It effectively displaced God as

29. Surin, *Freedom Not Yet*, 24.

30. Ibid.

31. Ibid.

32. See Surin, *Freedom Not Yet*, 25: "the reason that grounds the subject is not a reason

the secure ontological ground of the subject and subsequently justified the subject's independence and freedom. Kant paved the way for freedom to be defined as the unconstrained capacity to exercise one's will. However, Kant carefully qualified this notion of freedom by placing it within the limits of Reason. He knew that the unchecked exercise of individual will would result in a tyranny, so he maintained that individual freedom and a free society were possible only as long as the subject adhered to the dictates of Reason. Moreover, Kant held that in the public and political sphere freedom was further constrained by "universal law" as determined by the "general will of the people." He wrote, "The highest task which nature has set for mankind must therefore be that of establishing a society in which *freedom under external laws* would be combined to the greatest possible extent with irresistible force, in other words, of establishing a perfectly *just civil constitution.*"[33] Ultimately, Kantian transcendental philosophy paved the way for the "political emergence of the republican citizen who from 1789 onward (though a good case can be made for including 1776 in this periodization) would supplant the subject/*subjectus* of the previous historical and philosophical epic."[34]

The emergence of the Citizen Subject corresponded with a new aesthetic orientation. As Eva Shaper observes, Kant became known as the "Father of Modern Aesthetics" because of his insights in the "Critique of Aesthetic Judgment," part one of his *Critique of Judgment.*[35] Kant sought to uncover the principles of aesthetic judgment, which he conceived in terms of taste. Shaper explains, "In much eighteenth century usage, to be a person of taste was to be a person of independent judgment based on individual conviction, not on slavishly following rules. Kant is aware of this usage, and it is part of the aim of his analysis to secure a grounding of the judgment of taste in something that, as the personal, namely individual feeling, can carry the weight of an implied claim to autonomy."[36] This emphasis on

---

that can be specified within the terms of the activity of the subject: this reason is the basis of this subject's very possibility qua subject, and by virtue of that, reason is necessarily exterior to the activity of the thinking subject. Reason in this kind of employment is thus the activity of a single and universal quintessence whose object is reason itself, so that reason has necessarily to seek its ground within itself, as Hegel noted. Reason, by virtue of its self-grounding, is perforce the writing of the Absolute."

33. Kant, "Idea for a Universal History with a Cosmopolitan Purpose," 45–46.

34. Surin, *Freedom Not Yet,* 24.

35. Shaper, "Taste, Sublimity, and Genius," 368.

36. Ibid. 371–72.

autonomy means that the subject has "an attitude of wonder toward the world, and he who feels it *does not selfishly seek to possess the objects of his pleasure: he appreciates and appraises them.*"[37] The modern museum exemplifies this Kantian ideal. In the museum the subject sets his gaze upon art in order to appreciate, appraise, and contemplate, but he never tries to possess the aesthetic image, nor does it cultivate in him the desire to consume. By virtue of his rational outlook, the subject separates his desire from the influence of the image.

By the end of the nineteenth century, the metaphysical constitution of the Citizen Subject had fallen under critical attack. Since Nietzsche, philosophy has taken a decidedly postmetaphysical turn, and in the twentieth century Heidegger, Foucault, Derrida, and many others have all taken aim at metaphysics by deconstructing transcendental notions of reason and truth. Surin observes that this deconstruction corresponds to a "postpolitical conjecture" where sheer assertion and will to power characterize politics. He says, "As a result of the intervention represented by Nietzsche, truth, goodness, and beauty, that is, the guiding transcendental notions for the constitution of this epistemological and moral-political subject, are henceforth to be regarded merely as the functions and ciphers of supervening will to power."[38] This makes the actual operation of democracy very difficult, because once the demos no longer values the ideals of reason and truth, politics ceases to be by the people, for the people. Instead, politics becomes the constant cajoling of the electorate by professional politicians who are always campaigning. The distinct seasons of election and governance have completely morphed into one another. Today every act of governance is measured in light of its political effects over the electorate as politicians continually jockey for power. Governing *is* campaigning and campaigning *is* governing.

Another consequence of the postpolitical situation is the influence of corporations in politics. Surin writes,

> Today's regime of capitalist accumulation and the neoliberal and neoconservative ideologies identified with its current ascendancy simply have no need for the classical Citizen Subject . . . The disciples of Milton Friedman and Leo Strauss who today control the U.S. government's elite do not give a hoot about substantive notions of an informed and involved citizenry . . . it is virtually undeniable, especially in a time which is seeing the beginnings of an

37. Ibid. My italics.

38. Surin, *Freedom Not Yet*, 26.

economic crisis whose scale is becoming comparable to the great
crash of 1929, that corporations and markets have gained hugely
in legitimacy and power at the expense of the now deracinated
Citizen Subject.[39]

The market influences politics in two important ways. First, politicians are
constantly in need of funding for their campaigns. Once in office, the interests of their greatest donors inevitably influence their decisions and affect
public policy. Second, the market undercuts the transcendental notion of
freedom (which Kant understood as the capacity to exercise one's will in
accordance with reason and the law) by socializing subjects to experience
their democratic freedom as the liberty of desire and limitless consumption. Whereas the Citizen Subject understands his sovereignty as based
in the moral high ground of transcendental notions of right and duty, the
Consumer Subject feels entitled and regards himself as accountable only to
his own happiness. Moreover, the market socializes the Consumer Subject
with a particular aesthetic sensibility that is the opposite of the transcendental ideal. For Kant, the subject "does *not* selfishly seek to possess the
objects of his pleasure: he appreciates and appraises them"; the Consumer
Subject, however, is socialized by the seductive images of the market to
want what he sees, to possess the objects of his desire. These can be physical
things, images, people, places, ideas—virtually anything can be rendered a
consumable object.

Surin observes that the demise of the Citizen Subject "makes more
urgent the question of the ontological status of its putative successor, that
is, the subject of this postpolitical politics."[40] In other words, the loss of
transcendental metaphysics raises the question of what new ontological
basis can be found for a corresponding political subjectivity. Although he
laments the death of transcendental metaphysics, Surin sees no point in
returning to the bygone Enlightenment era. The way forward, he says, must
eschew metaphysics and presume a radically immanent ontology. Rather
than appeal to Truth or Reason, he proposes a "Scotist-Spinozist-Deleuzean
ontology" that "posits an infinity of expressivities and their associated possible worlds in a way that is at once rigorously immanent and materialist,
and also rigorously politicized."[41] This ontology looks to the sheer power of
human life as a liberating force against the oppression of capitalism. "With-

39. Ibid., 30–31.
40. Ibid., 28.
41. Ibid., 237.

out being transcendent (there being no universal subject and universal object for it to transcend), this ontology serves as a transcendental field for the becoming of new multiplicities, each new multiplicity being potentially another name for a new kind of political agent living for a liberation that the old sovereignties are now unable to forestall."[42]

For Surin "infinite multiplicity" is an alternative to both transcendental metaphysics and theological metaphysics because these options attempt in their respective ways to secure political order by appealing to Transcendence. Whereas theology appeals to God, modernity appeals to Reason, but each positions the social order in relation to an exterior Other in order to secure notions of truth, goodness, and beauty from which to derive universal laws and civil society. Surin argues that any appeal to a metaphysical other is philosophically untenable and unnecessary. He is pragmatic in seeking an ontology that has *not* been abstracted from the material processes of consumption and production, but is rather constituted *as* resistance to capitalist oppression. Although his ontology is essentially antagonistic, it is not merely negative because in its resistance it unleashes "the infinity of expressivities and their associated possible worlds."[43] Infinite multiplicity can always find a new horizon and renewed energy for freedom, "each new multiplicity being potentially another name for a new kind of political agent living for a liberation . . ."[44]

Surin's immanent ontology represents one side of an important debate that has emerged in recent years about the relationship between metaphysics and political subjectivity. Whereas Surin and other Marxist theorists, such as Antonio Negri and Michael Hardt, advocate for an absolutely immanent ontology, some Christian theologians—John Milbank, D. Stephen Long, Conor Cunningham, William Desmond, and other scholars associated with Radical Orthodoxy—have articulated a postsecular ontology that boldly reclaims theological metaphysics as the only suitable ground for political subjectivity. Like Surin, these scholars recognize that we now find ourselves in a postpolitical era characterized by mere assertion and will to power. For example, Long says that the only truth to be found in modern politics is that "power alone can bind people together."[45] Although Surin and Long agree on the degraded status of contemporary politics, they

42. Ibid.

43. Ibid.

44. Ibid.

45. Long, *Speaking of God*, 262

diverge on the relationship between politics and metaphysics. Whereas Surin abandons the hope of any metaphysical foundation for truth, Long argues that the most fundamental political question before us is "how to subordinate power to truth and goodness."[46] For Long, "politics and metaphysics go together" because "once we no longer ask the questions of the transcendentals—'What is good?' 'What is truth?' 'What is it to be?'—then we will get an impoverished politics." Long argues that politics needs metaphysics and metaphysics needs the "specificities of Christian doctrine."[47] Specifically, politics needs a participatory metaphysics that wrests political and social life from the jaws of nihilism. This entails the rejection of Kant's policing of the sublime in favor of a Thomistic doctrine of *analogia entis*. From the vantage point of Radical Orthodoxy, Kant's policing of the sublime is merely the culmination of scholastic metaphysics and not the overcoming of it. Through a Thomistic theology of participation, Radical Orthodoxy offers an alternative to the ill-begotten legacy of Kantian metaphysics on the one hand and the immanent ontology of neo-Marxist political theory on the other (Surin, Hardt, Negri, et al.). This alternative means that Long and proponents of Radical Orthodoxy are both "for and against postmodernity."[48] On the one hand, postmodern scholars (including Marxist scholars) have correctly diagnosed modern metaphysics as a problem, but on the other hand their wholesale rejection of metaphysics leaves us without the ability to answer questions such as "What is good?" and "What is truth?" and "What is it to be?"

The debate between Marxist scholars and Radical Orthodoxy regarding an ontological ground for political subjectivity has been illuminating, but it has up until now neglected an important question. Both sides more or less agree that modern transcendentalism has been thoroughly deconstructed, but what new metaphysic has emerged to fill the void left by modern transcendentalism? Now that transcendentalism is gone (and with it the Citizen Subject), what is the metaphysical basis of the newly minted Consumer Subject?

46. Ibid.

47. Ibid.

48. See Long, "Radical Orthodoxy." Long further states: "Because modern transcendentalism rendered a world where God was irrelevant, radical orthodoxy finds a momentary ally in postmodern deconstruction . . . But the alliance between postmodernity and radical orthodoxy can be at most momentary, for, like modern philosophers, most postmodern thinkers cannot find their way back to the roots to remember them. The roots have for them no 'proper name.' In fact these roots are *not*" (129).

This question assumes that despite the philosophical claims about the end of metaphysics, metaphysics is integral to social life today. The religious desire to commune with transcendence is evident in modern spectacle entertainments. Vampires, superheroes, magical beings, and fantastic worlds of all sorts appear often in movies and other popular entertainments because the metaphysical imagination is alive and well. Virtual realities offer another way to escape finitude and the limits of mortal embodiment. As an avatar, the subject can approximate himself as a transcendent being, and such a possibility has obvious and widespread appeal. Thus, it is presumptuous to think that the critiques of postmodern philosophy have somehow resulted in the eradication of metaphysics. Humanity is fundamentally religious and will inevitably seek communion with one form of transcendence or another.

Religious longing persists not because humanity has failed to progress, but because we are insatiably curious. We return again to search for what transcends us, because no question is more ultimate than the question of the Ultimate. William Desmond observes that questions about God occur "in astonishment and perplexity":

> astonishment before the sheer givenness of being; perplexity about the intelligibility, the meaning, indeed goodness of that given being . . . For the question of God does not arise in the determinate cognition of a definite matter of fact about which we are curious. It concerns more our metaphysical astonishment before the givenness of the being-there of being, also our perplexity as to what it might all mean, in relation to origin and end, what the point of it all is in relation to its worthiness to be affirmed as good.[49]

The search for God is not merely cognitive but proceeds from the core of our being, and it is expressed in our desires and longings. It corresponds with what Desmond describes as the *passio essendi*, which names the "primal ethos of being" and our astonishment at the sheer gift of life.[50] We are *given to be* before we *endeavor to be*, and this gift calls us into a search for being in excess of ourselves.[51] This search opens us to the mindfulness of transcendence as we look for signs, pray, search for analogies, and seek out ecstatic experiences. It can lead us into the doors of the cathedral whose vaulted ceilings and stained glass windows draw our gaze up and indicate

49. Desmond, *God and the Between*, 19–20.

50. Ibid.

51. Ibid., 34.

the Transcendence and otherness of the triune God. At apprehending God we may kneel quietly in prayer or shout "Hallelujah!" and realize the gifts of grace and salvation. Alternately, our search for God may lead us astray and put us in the grip of a malicious transcendence, a malevolent metaphysics, which corrupts our innate desire for God by turning it into a desire to consume. This metaphysics merely *approximates* communion with God and can only pretend to satisfy our deepest longings. This is why things consumed in the society of the spectacle are disposable; consumer culture incessantly promises us experiences of rapture, but all it provides is an insatiable desire. The cathedrals of the society of the spectacle—Times Square, New York; Shinjuku District, Tokyo; Las Vegas, Nevada—draw our gaze *not* to God but to the transcendences portrayed in the entertainments and shopping malls of consumer culture.

James K. A. Smith argues that the many aspects of consumer culture constitute liturgies that form subjects much as formal religious liturgies do. These liturgies of consumer culture "encourage us to accept a certain magic, the myth that the garments and equipment that circulate from the mall through our homes and into the landfill simply emerged in shops as if dropped by aliens."[52] Moreover, "the liturgy of consumption births in us a desire for a way of life that is destructive of creation itself . . . it births in us a desire for a way of life that we can't feasibly extend to others, creating a system of privilege and exploitation. In short, the only way for this vision of this kingdom to be reality is if we keep it to ourselves."[53]

No society can afford to ignore the metaphysical ideals that shape the desires and longings of its citizens, for this can have profound implications for social life and political discourse. Understanding the relationship between metaphysics and politics produces a wiser political theory than mere immanence can produce. Desmond contends that "the loss of the beyond of metaphysics, as going with the immanent absolutization of the political, tends to lead to the loss of the wisdom of the immanent that is the genuine art of the political."[54] There is wisdom in immanence, but it requires not "exhausting politics with immanence" but being open to the ways in which politics can point us beyond the here and now. Desmond says, "Clearly our care for the excellences of immanence will be different when one has the intimation that there is more at stake than a self-sufficient immanence,

52. Smith, *Desiring the Kingdom*, 101.
53. Ibid.
54. Desmond, "Neither Sovereignty nor Servility," 156.

when signs of something beyond have entered one's sense of the equivo-
cal play of immanent powers, and not only the temptations of tyranny
that we know here but also what is good now."[55] Metaphysics is essential
to politics because it can help discern and counteract false transcendences
that have gripped culture and society. Thus, Desmond cautions: "a hidden
metaphysics can influence how we think of politics, just as certain political
arrangements can either hinder or enable a genuine metaphysical openness
of mind. What happens in the apparently empty ether of thought may come
down to earth, and a masked metaphysics come to walk the streets—or
stalk. For monsters too might float in the Empyrean, coming to earth with
gifts glittering and poisoned."[56]

What "masked metaphysic" has filled the void left by the deconstruction of the Citizen Subject? What malicious transcendence now walks the
streets with gifts glittering and poisoned? The metaphysic operating in
the modern society of the spectacle is the same one that was pervasive in
Rome's spectacle entertainments. Augustine described it as the worship of
demons. For Rome, spectacle involved both entertainment and the formal
worship of pagan gods. As discussed in the previous chapter, Augustine recognized these gods as nothing—mere handicrafts—but he also realized that
the idols and images of paganism were powerful and effective mediators of
social and political life. He maintained that these images made humanity
vulnerable to a demonic metaphysics. For Augustine, demons were beings
situated between immanence and transcendence. Like God, they possessed
"an immortal body, like the bodies on high, but with a diseased soul, like
those below."[57] Because they possessed a diseased soul, "the mind of the
demons is in subjection to the *passions of desire*."[58] Having both perfect,
immortal bodies and insatiable desire, demons were beings of limitless capacity for wicked passions of the soul. They were consumers *par excellence*.

Augustine said that Romans admired demons for their composite being and regarded them as mediators between humanity and God. However,
against the Romans, Augustine argued that Roman admiration of the demonic ideal was really misdirected longing for God: it is not demons who
mediate between God and humanity, but Christ. Whereas a demon is a
mere composite of human passions and divinity (i.e., a diseased soul and

---

55. Ibid., 157
56. Ibid., 153.
57. Augustine, *City of God* 9.17 (Bettenson, 364).
58. Ibid., 9.6 (Bettenson, 350).

immortal body), Christ is *fully* human and *fully* divine. However, in his humanity Christ was not subject to sinful passions, and in divinity he was embodied, which is why Augustine argues that Christ is not only human- ity's Mediator but also its Savior. The hypostatic union is an alternative to the demonic metaphysics of paganism, and the Christian participates in this alternative metaphysics by partaking in the Eucharist. Whereas con- sumption proper to the demons only results in insatiable desire, consuming the Eucharist unites the believer with Christ's sacramental body and blood. Moreover, it unites him with the ecclesial body of Christ.

Augustine's understanding of the demonic and his understanding of the Incarnation as an alternative metaphysics is critical for Christian en- gagement with the modern society of the spectacle, because the demonic ideal is a powerful force shaping the imagination of the Consumer Sub- ject. The images displayed by the society of the spectacle in its marketing campaigns and entertainment venues project the demonic ideal as some- thing to be admired and imitated. Consider the marketing campaigns of Abercrombie and Fitch, Victoria's Secret, and Dolce and Gabbana (to name but a few examples). The bodies portrayed there are not real bodies, but transcendent bodies that are perfect, immortal, and dripping with the pas- sions of the soul (lust, greed, and insatiable desire.) Their ubiquity ensures their full integration into consumer culture's symbolic order and into the social imagination of the populace. Alternately, consider the vampires made popular by the *Twilight* series and in many other movies and televi- sion shows that have captivated the imaginations of young people (and also many adults). These beings are quintessential demons. They also are be- ings of insatiable desire who possess immortal and perfect bodies and who occupy a space between immanence and transcendence. Finally, consider the ongoing fascination with superheroes and superhero blockbusters that have captivated American audiences. These beings are hybrid beings who exemplify what Augustine described as the topsy-turvy quality of the de- mons: their bodies are perfectly strong and immortal, yet they are inflamed with the passions of the soul. Taken together, these images and narratives function as an iconography that reflects a demonic ideal, which consumer culture admires and, in various ways, aspires to obtain. This demonic ideal is the "metaphysical subtlety" that Debord sensed but failed to identify spe- cifically when he wrote *Society of the Spectacle*.

The prevalence of the demonic ideal indicates that the challenges con- fronting Christianity today are analogous to those that confronted early Christianity. First, we are dealing with Empire (and many scholars have articulated the various ways in which this is the case), and second, the Empire confronting us is, like Rome, a society of the spectacle saturated with a demonic metaphysics. In order to engage the society of the spectacle, we must have a nuanced understanding of how its perverse iconography cultivates desire.

Marketing, Demons, and the Double Consciousness of the Image

In his insightful book *What Do Pictures Want?*, W. J. T. Mitchell observes that marketers often appeal to notions of autonomy and individuality in order to manipulate the subject. As an example, Mitchell examines a typical Sprite commercial called "Moviemakers," which is an ironic anti-commercial that promotes a product by making fun of marketing and advertising. The opening scene portrays several marketers engaged in a brainstorming session. They are anxious and ready to share an exciting new way of branding products with their producer. When the producer enters the room to inquire about their cutting-edge idea, they present him with the "Death Slug." The ridiculous "Death Slug" amounts to an eighteen-inch tube of bright green slime, which they proceed to throw across the room at the nearest window. Thrilled at the site of the Death Slug sliding down the window, they explain its power as a brand: it can appear alongside an infinite number of tie-ins—slug slippers, a slug rap video, slug tacos, slug-on-a-stick snacks. The producer, who wants to use every possible means of reaching the consumer, is impressed with the array of applications for the Death Slug, but he asks, "This is nice but what about the movie?" The marketers answer with an air or of smug superiority: "Well, we haven't got a script yet, but we can bang one out by Friday." As the Death Slug continues to slide down the window, leaving a trail of green ooze in its path, the screen fades to black and a disembodied voice tells the viewer, "Don't buy the Hollywood hype. Buy what *you* want." This is followed by the image of a bottle of Sprite, which is presented as an object of sublime desire. Finally, a slogan appears that reads, "Image is nothing, Thirst is everything. Obey your thirst."

The Moviemakers commercial is obviously an advertisement posing as an anti-commercial that plays on the consumer's awareness of marketing manipulation. Mitchell insightfully observes that it presents the soft drink "as the Real Thing, the object of authentic desire." The ironic moral is: crave what *you, the consumer*, want and not what the image-makers want you to have. Desire is an essential aspect of marketing, and the Moviemakers commercial illustrates how marketers manufacture desire as an expression of the consumer's identity and autonomy. Images often play an important role in the production of desire. Mitchell observes that images are characterized by the "juxtaposition of *image* and *thirst*, the visual and the oral—in Jacques Lacan's terms, the scopic and the vocative drives."[59] They share this characteristic in common with Rome's spectacle entertainments. The ancient spectacles of the Coliseum and the spectacles of modern advertising focus the subject's gaze to create an insatiable desire that keeps the subject coming back again and again. In order to illustrate this commonality, in the following table I have set Mitchell's description of the use of images in modern marketing next to Augustine's description of Alypius in Rome's Coliseum:

MODERN MARKETING	THE ROMAN COLISEUM
"The surprising discovery is that images [of modern marketing] operate even more powerfully in the oral than the optical channel: that is to say, *we do not merely see pictures, we drink in their images with our eyes* (Shakespeare called them 'blind mouths'). And pictures in turn have a tendency to swallow us up, or (as the expression goes) take us in. But images are also, notoriously, a drink that fails to satisfy our thirst. Their main function is to awaken desire; to create, not gratify thirst; to provoke a sense of lack and cravings by giving us the apparent presence of something and taking it away in the same gesture."[60] —Mitchell, *What Do Pictures Want?*	"[Alypius] saw the blood and *he gulped* the brutality along with it; he did not turn away but *fixed his gaze* there and *drank in the frenzy* . . . not aware of what he was doing . . . intoxicated on sanguinary pleasure. No longer was he the man who had joined the crowd; he was now one of the crowd he had joined, and a genuine companion of those who had led him there. He watched . . . lured back again . . . dragging others."[61] —Augustine, *Confessions*

59. Mitchel, *What Do Pictures Want?* 80.

60. Ibid.

61. Augustine, *Confessions* 6.9.13 (Boulding, 109).

Augustine describes Alypius as violated by the spectacle. Through the corruption of his desire he lost sight of his convictions and became just "one of the crowd," going back again and again in order to try to satisfy the craving that spectacle had created within him. Whereas Augustine recognized that Alypius had been manipulated by spectacle, the modern Consumer Subject does not recognize that his desires have been coerced. When he enters the shopping mall, for example, his desire is cultivated, but he does not perceive this assault on his desires because he is deluded by his sense of autonomy. Surrounded by spectacles designed to cultivate his desire, the shopper chooses from an endless array of products and offerings, and he regards his choices as an exercise of his freedom. His desire to consume is, he thinks, an expression of his authentic self. His desires tell him who he is, and the market is at its most profitable and powerful when it makes room for every possible desire. It embraces diversity, pluralism, difference, and tolerance because these liberal values make it possible to realize every person as a desiring subject. The market levels all social and cultural distinctions by dispensing with any value that would limit the cultivation and consummation of desire. As David Bentley Hart observes,

> The market thrives on a desire that recognizes no commonality of needs, a desire that seeks to consume and to create an identity out of what it consumes, a desire that produces out of its own energy and in indifference to a shared proportion of the good that might limit invention or acquisition. A desire that expands to the limits of which it is capable: not an analogical desire for God or the other but a desire for nothing as such, producing in order to desire more. Here one sees the necessary if not always immediately apparent synonymy of consumerism and nihilism: in our "society of the spectacle" (to use Guy Debord's phrase), the open field where arbitrary choices may be made among indifferently desirable objects must be cleared and then secured against the disruptions of the Good; this society must presume, and subtly advocate, the nonexistence of any higher "value" than choice, any truth that might order desire toward a higher end; desire may posit, seize, want, not want—but it must not obey.[62]

Mitchell observes that images play a powerful role in shaping and cultivating consumer desire, and he observes that the images of modern marketing are very similar to the images of ancient religion. For ancient peoples, images and idols were powerful ways of communing with Transcendence

62. Hart, *Beauty of the Infinite*, 433–34.

and cultivating a longing for immortality. They provide a similar function today. Mitchell says, "I believe that magical attitudes toward images are just as powerful in the modern world as they were in so-called ages of faith. I also believe that the ages of faith were a bit more skeptical than we give them credit for."[63] He also observes that the capacity of images to function as idols or icons is "not something that we 'get over' when we grow up, become modern, or acquire critical consciousness."[64] Like Mitchell, John Ralston Saul argues that despite pretensions of progress and enlightenment, modernity did not eradicate the religious and metaphysical power of the image:

> Until the simultaneous beginnings of the Age of Reason and the Renaissance, this craft [of making images] played a social, political, and above all metaphysical or religious role. From the fifteenth century on . . . the idea of art began to quietly separate itself from craft. By the eighteenth century the divorce was more or less formal, although there have been regular attempts to reunite the two. In the early nineteenth century, museums were created for the sole purpose of aesthetic enjoyment. The idea that art is its own reason for existence has now been so firmly established that few people would question it.
>
> *And yet it is improbable that the image, which has played such a fundamentally religious or magical role for more than fifteen thousand years, could simply be freed of itself in the space of a few centuries to become a mere object of art.*[65]

The modern attempt to contain the power of the image by conceiving of it as art has only made us ignorant of the religious and metaphysical power that the image continues to have in social life. Saul suggests that "the death of God combined with the perfection of the image has brought us to a whole new state of expectation . . . that image has all the Godly powers . . . The electronic image is man as God and the ritual involved leads us not to a mysterious Holy Trinity but back to ourselves. In the absence of a clear understanding that we are now the only source, these images cannot help but return to the expression of magic and fear proper to idolatrous societies."[66] Ultimately, modernity has not produced a secular, rational society that understands itself as the only source of existence; rather, it has

63. Mitchell, *What Do Pictures Want?* 8.

64. Ibid.

65. Saul, *Voltaire's Bastards*, 426. My italics.

66. Ibid., 460.

produced an idolatrous society in which the power of the image-as-idol plays a significant role in cultivating desire and molding it around the processes of production and consumption.

Mitchell observes that the relationship between people, images, and idolatry has always been complex and characterized by a "double consciousness."[67] On the one hand, we are conscious that images are nothing, and today we often regard them as such. In our technological society, in which producing images is often easier than producing text, images are commonplace. On the other hand, we find ourselves glued to the screen and captivated by images of disaster, eroticism, excess, drama, violence, and suspense. Images may make us stagger at beauty or shudder at horror, or they may compel us to deeper contemplation. Whether they are still or cinematic, they have remarkable power to compel us. Mitchell contends that "images have the capacity to be everything *because* they are also nothing." Images lack substance and thereby draw us into their void, and when this happens, we experience desire and transfer desire to the object to which they refer us. We respond as if the thing they depict is what we need to fill the void they create. Thus, images have the power to reframe and recontextualize the world. They cause us to feel and think differently about our lives and circumstances as if they were independent *beings in their own right*. Mitchell observes that this capacity of the image is the common denominator between images as advertising and images as religious idols:

> Every advertising executive knows that some images, to use the trade jargon, "have legs"—that is, they seem to have a surprising capacity to generate new directions and surprising twists in an ad campaign, as if they had an intelligence and purposiveness of their own. When Moses demands that Aaron explain the making of the golden calf, Aaron says that he merely threw the Israelites' gold jewelry into the fire "and this calf came out" (Exod. 32:23 [KJV]), as if it were a self-created automaton. Evidently some idols have legs too. The idea that images have a kind of social or psychological power of their own is, in fact, the reigning cliché of contemporary visual culture . . . If there is a commonplace in contemporary image theory, in fact, it is that images (if not works of art) today are credited with a power undreamt of by the ancient idolaters and their iconoclastic opponents.[68]

67. Ibid.

68. Mitchell, *What Do Pictures Want?* 31, 96.

Mitchell takes the notion that images "have legs" one step further by suggesting that "what pictures want from us, what we have failed to give them, is an ideal of visuality adequate to their *ontology*." He contends that we must recognize that images are "living things . . . not just passive entities that coexist with human hosts."[69] Although Mitchell sees images as ontological, he recognizes the significant difficulties associated with this premise. Should we really regard images as beings in their own right? Are they really "living things"?[70] He asks, "Why does the link between images and living things seem so inevitable and necessary, at the same time that it almost invariably arouses a kind of disbelief: 'Do you really *believe* that images want things?' My answer is, no, I don't believe it. But we cannot ignore that human beings (including myself) insist on talking and behaving as if they *did* believe it, and that is what I mean by the 'double consciousness' surrounding images."[71]

Early Christianity provides us with insight into the dilemma Mitchell identifies, because the observation that we exhibit a double consciousness about images echoes early Christian thinking about paganism and idolatry. Although early Christians regarded the idols and images of Roman religion as nothing but mere handicrafts, they also recognized that the images and idols of pagan religion exhibited an extraordinary power to shape desire. Augustine regarded the subject as a worshiping *habitus* comprised of desires, thoughts, reasons, attitudes, and behaviors that either directed the subject toward God or toward a malicious metaphysics. Images could function either as icons, thereby facilitating communion with God, or as idols, thereby cultivating human desires in accord with transcendent evil. Thus, Augustine said that pagan idols were imbued with the power of "demons which some strange art has attached to idols by means of the fetters of their own passions." [72] In other words, the image cultivated passions within the subject that subsequently functioned as a doorway between the subject and a transcendent evil. He implored the Romans to realize that their idols had taken hold of their passion and desires and urged them to refrain from this "wicked art":

> For the fact that man was the maker of his gods did not mean that
> he was not possessed by what he had made, for by worshipping

69. Ibid., 92.

70. Ibid., 47. My italics.

71. Ibid., 11.

72. Augustine, *City of God* 8.24 (Bettenson, 336).

them he was drawn into fellowship with them, and I do not mean fellowship with senseless idols, but with crafty demons . . . the unclean spirits, bound to these images by this wicked art, had brought the souls of their worshippers into a wretched captivity, by forcing them into their fellowship. Hence the Apostle says, *"We know that an idol is nothing; when the gentiles offer sacrifice, it is to demons that they sacrifice, not to God. I do not want you to enter into fellowship with demons"* [1 Cor 10:20].[73]

Augustine's assessment of pagan worship as "fellowship with demons" illuminates a way around the dilemma that Mitchell describes as the double consciousness of the image. We experience images as "living things" because images have the capacity to make us mindful of transcendent ontology and cultivate our desire to commune with a higher order of being. This is why images have traditionally been used as icons to help worshipers commune with God. Today, however, the power of the image resides with advertisers, who have mastered the art of representing consumable goods as transcendent objects. The consumer participates *analogically* in the transcendence depicted by the image by possessing the product it depicts. This process of seduction constitutes an act of worship. The consumer is a worshiper, the image operates as a *modus significandi,* and the advertiser who created the image is his priest. However, the consumer will ultimately find that this act of worship does not satiate his desire. He experiences this disappointment as continued or renewed desire to consume. The process repeats itself as he finds a new image and object of desire. Augustine shows us that such a person is captive to an ontology of *insatiable desire* that he describes as the "fellowship of the demons." The market is deeply invested in demonic ontology, which is exhibited in the way the market produces desire.

Augustine's insights into the metaphysics of demonic ontology correct William Cavanaugh's helpful but inadequate analysis of the market and consumer culture. Cavanaugh rightly suggests that the market is "a way of seeing the world, of reading its images and signs," but he accounts for the emptiness of consumer culture by suggesting that these signs and images "refer *only* to other signifiers, *not* to the signified."[74] In other words, Cavanaugh argues that consumer culture is a system of signifiers that fails to refer the subject to a genuine Transcendence (God), but instead refers the subject only to other signifiers. The implication is that the system of signi-

73. Ibid., 335–36.
74. Cavanaugh, *Being Consumed,* 69. My italics.

fiers we encounter in consumer culture operates on the immanent plane.[75] However, this is not the case. Advertisers have learned what religious traditions have known for centuries, which is that when images are employed as icons they have a remarkable power over the subject. They use this power to form the subject as a consumer, but in so doing they unknowingly refer him to a transcendent ontology of insatiable desire.

Spectacle and the De-intensification of Being

Gazing violence was an important part of spectacle entertainment in ancient Rome, and this is also true in the modern society of the spectacle. Although actual blood no longer stains the sandy floor of the Coliseum, virtual violence is an essential part of film, television, and video games. As John Milbank observes, our "modern society of the spectacle retreats from the pure liturgy of monotheism to a pagan theatricality. And like paganism, it invests its hopes in a controllable economy of violence: where this much and no more blood was once shed to appease the gods, now this much and no more simulated violence, or rather as much simulated violence as you like, will appease our 'aggressive urges' . . ."[76]

Modern technology provides for experiences of violence that operate on the order of the hyperreal. Virtual reality video games, for example, enable the gamer to engage in fantasies of mass murder and horror that would be impossible in the material world. Exceedingly violent video games have become the most profitable and popular entertainments of all time. Adrenaline courses through the gamer's veins as he dismembers, decapitates, disembowels, sets on fire and chops into little pieces his victims, who cry out in agony and beg for mercy. The gamer can also engage in explicit sex and pornography, and some games even experiment with virtual rape.[77] As Andrew Tuplin observes, "The implicit suggestion of these products is that, like gravity, morality does not necessarily exist in a virtual world. Morality

75. Cavanaugh may not intend this implication. However, if this is the case, then the question he has failed to answer is, If the significations of the market are not merely immanent, then to what transcendent ontology do they refer? Moreover, what is the nature of the transcendence they signify? I contend that the answer to this question is what Augustine helpfully describes as the demonic.

76. Milbank, *Being Reconciled,* 33.

77. For a helpful and interesting inquiry into the morality and ethics of violence in video games, see Tuplin, "Virtual Morality."

and consequence can be switched off. Anything goes." [78] This contributes to enormous sales and makes the video game industry very lucrative. For example, in 2011 a new record for the biggest entertainment release of all time (for any medium) was set by *Call of Duty: Modern Warfare 3*, which reportedly sold 6.5 million copies (grossing $400 million) in just twenty-four hours, ultimately surpassing the box office earnings of the *Star Wars* and *Lord of the Rings* films.[79]

The point of virtual violence is not simulating reality but *exceeding it* in order to provide the subject with experiences of a transcendent meta-physics where the limitations of mortality and the constraints of morality vanish. Although virtual reality is a phenomenon of the modern era, using technology to produce experiences of transcendence is at least as old as Roman paganism. As noted in the previous chapter, Roman paganism used elaborate apparatuses to provide worshipers with spectacular experiences of communion with divinities. New converts saw pagan gods by looking "through a glass darkly," and pagan priests utilized devices such as temple doors opened by unseen mechanisms that would magically reveal the god or goddess. Underground piping at Corinth magically turned water into wine. All of this required technical expertise. Pagan priests were techni-cians and operators of these technologies who learned their skills through special manuals and training. Like today's virtual reality, their special ef-fects were designed to give the worshiper a spectacle and intensification of being. The hyperreality that the gamer experiences through violent video games momentarily heightens his sense of being, but, like a drug addict coming down from a high, he inevitably experiences a de-intensification. As John Milbank observes, "the situation of pure spectacle is a recreational relaxation precisely as a diminution of life, or its real interactive excite-ments, its real consummations and overwhelmings by power . . . It follows that the circumstance of spectacle is a de-intensification of being."[80]

The cycle of de-intensification of being not only characterizes violent video games, but is endemic and emblematic of the whole society of the spectacle. For example, when a consumer enters the shopping mall, her senses are engaged by a panoply of stimuli designed to intoxicate. Images, music, scents, and products swirl together in a whirlwind of desire. The consumer does not have to want anything before entering the shopping mall

78. Ibid.

79. Richmond, "*Call of Duty: Modern Warfare 3* Breaks Sales Record," par. 6.

80. Milbank, *Being Reconciled*, 31.

because it is designed to cultivate desire *for her,* and it provides her with the products she needs to consummate the desire *it* has produced. However, once the consumer leaves the shopping mall—with products in hand—the effect of the shopping mall's spectacles begins to wear off. The products that once seemed so appealing gradually lose their gloss and sheen. One day she will peer into her overflowing closet and conclude, "I have nothing to wear." Taken literally, this statement is nonsensical; what she really means is that the clothes she purchased in the past no longer provide her with the intensification of being that she craves. Purse in hand, she heads off once again to the shopping mall, and the cycle of de-intensification begins anew.

The consumption of popular music also exhibits this cycle of de-intensification. The typical pop song has a shelf life of weeks or months; soon another hit song displaces it. The typical teenager finds rapture and even moments of ecstasy in popular music and music videos, but his iPod or MP3 player is full of songs and video clips that he has used up. They no longer provide him with the intensification of being he constantly seeks, so he is always on the search for the next song that will provide him with the high he is looking for.

Video games, popular music, and shopping are but three examples of how the cycle of de-intensification is integral to modern spectacle entertainment. The cycle that produces de-intensification of being is a byproduct of how the market positions the subject in the place of objectification. Like a spectator in the Coliseum, the Consumer Subject has no attachment to the objects of his gaze. To have no attachment to the objects of one's gaze was the seduction of Rome's spectacle entertainments. The spectator sat safely above the death and mayhem of the arena floor. This provided him with an experience of transcendence. Like a demigod, he looked down with no regard for the suffering of mortals. In the modern society of the spectacle, the Consumer Subject *rises* above the material world by means of his purchasing power. He can buy and discard at will, because for him everything material is dispensable and replaceable. Cavanaugh observes that consumer culture is characterized by "a detachment from the things we buy. Our relationships with products tend to be short-lived: rather than hoarding treasured objects, consumers are characterized by a constant dissatisfaction with material goods."[81] Consumption is the modern means of transcending immanence. Again, through his purchasing power, the consumer is able to rise above the material world and experience himself

81. Cavanaugh, *Being Consumed,* 35.

as a transcendent being. He does not rise as high as God—for God is not imprisoned by the passions of the soul—but he rises high enough to occupy the space between immanence and transcendence that Augustine calls the fellowship of the demons. In this space he is like the demons in that he is both captive to the passions of the soul and detached from material reality. However, he can only maintain this state momentarily and intermittently, because the realities of material embodiment break in on his consciousness. Sickness, death, limited resources, and all the trappings of immanence drag him back to earth. This process has a numbing effect on the consumer, and so ever-greater spectacles must be produced to keep the Consumer Subject engaged. Images must be more vivid, violence even more excessive, reality television more outrageous, political campaigns more dramatic, and so on. This leads to the overall denegration of society. As Desmond observes, "It is our will to elevation that produces our degradation. We do not throw ourselves down, rather we seek to be our own self-creating source of full transcendence, but the lack in our erotic will to be thus sovereign turns back into itself and becomes subject to its own void."[82]

Eucharist as Redirected Gaze

In his crucifixion, Jesus of Nazareth allowed himself to become a spectacle and an object of consumption. He said, "Take, eat, this is my body broken for you, my blood shed for you." Augustine taught that the body of Christ was the "true spectacle" and object of human desire. There are three important implications of this teaching that juxtapose the consumption of the modern society of the spectacle with the consumption of the Eucharist:

1. Whereas consumption in the society of the spectacle is characterized by *detachment*, the Eucharist *unites* the subject with the body and blood of Christ.

2. Whereas the society of the spectacle affirms the Consumer Subject as autonomous and self-ruling, the Eucharist signifies the believer's absolute dependence on God and need for salvation.

3. Whereas the society of the spectacle is a system of signifiers that refer the Consumer Subject to a demonic metaphysics, the Eucharist signifies the believer's participation in the hypostatic union. He is united to Christ in death and in eternal life. Through Christ's death and

82. Desmond, *God and the Between*, 257.

resurrection the believer finds the true object of his longing. More-over, it initiates a new political subjectivity because the sacramental body of Christ binds him to the ecclesial body of Christ.

It is also important to recognize that participation in the Eucharist requires the cultivation of a *new metaphysical vision*. One must learn to see the body and blood in the elements of the sacrament. Ambrose taught his catechu-mens, "You must not trust, then, wholly to your bodily eyes; that which is not seen is more really seen, for the object of sight is temporal, but that other eternal, which is not apprehended by the eye, but is discerned by the mind and spirit."[83] The difficulty for the Consumer Subjects of today's Western democracies is that their gaze has been trained by the images and idols of the society of the spectacle to desire not Christ but the allure of de-monic metaphysics. In other words, the problem is *not* merely the inability to see beyond the limits of immanent reality (i.e., to see that it is possible for the material elements of the sacrament to exceed themselves according to a sacramental logic); rather, the problem is that the Consumer Subject is already a disciple of a more seductive metaphysics. He is under the influ-ence of the demonic, because in the society of the spectacle one learns to see with what Hart calls the optics of the market: "The market, then, is a particular optics, a particular order of vision . . . The particular pathology of the market in consequence is a kind of anesthesia through inanition of the apparent, a painless and wonderless gaze, prey to moments of anxiety but immune to awe."[84]

The Christian does not see the world through the optics of the market, as a collection of consumable objects, because his desires correspond to an ontology articulated by the metaphysics of the Eucharist. The Christian participates analogically in Christ's death and resurrection by consuming his body and blood. This analogical participation mediates his desire and transforms what it means to consume Jesus' body and blood. Whereas the gaze of the consumer metaphorically drinks in the object of his desire and renders it void, the Christian sees with a vision that "breaks down the rigid lineaments of a world that interprets itself principally according to the bril-liant glamour and spectacle of power . . . [Christian optics] is a way of see-ing that must be learned, because it alters every perspective upon things; and to learn it properly one must be conformed to what one sees. Vision

83. Ambrose, *On Mysteries* 3.15.
84. Hart, *Beauty of the Infinite*, 437.

here is inseparable, even indistinguishable from practice: faith, which is the form this Christian optics must take, lies in the surrender of one's actions to the form of Christ."[85]

Resisting Empire: Eucharist and Political Subjectivity

Ken Surin observes that as "a metaphysics of participation in the divine being" Christianity's remarkable advantage as a political ontology is its capacity to direct the subject's desire toward an absolute Other. He says, "Christianity is founded on a logic that affirms the rationality of a desire grounded in something beyond that which we know and desire, and to this extent it is ontologically disposed to acknowledge the exteriority pre-mised on self-surpassing desire, the desire that gets beyond what desire itself can know or anticipate. This is a truly remarkable ontological asset (if one can speak of it in this way), since it enables Christianity ceaselessly to move beyond the limits necessarily constituted by the given."[86] Christian-ity's "ontological asset" was a critical aspect of its resistance to the Roman Empire. The central act of Christian worship, Eucharist, not only expressed religious devotion but simultaneously served as the basis for an alterna-tive political community whose only allegiance was to Christ. Christ was made present to the worshiper in the sacramental body, in the Incarnate Body, and in the ecclesial body. As we observed in the last chapter, access to these various bodies required rigorous instruction and ritual purification, including exorcism, which was meant to protect him from the influence of the Roman state and demonic metaphysics. As a political subject, the Christian was metaphysically mediated, and this mediation was reinforced weekly through the liturgy. Christians refused to participate in the con-spicuous consumption (*analisken*) of Rome's spectacle entertainments, and their abstinence caused the Romans to revile them and regard them as a threat to the political order. According to Kyle, the first-century senator Tacitus considered Christians "guilty of 'hatred of mankind' in part because they shunned the pagan sacrifices and spectacles—the very things Romans saw as essential for integration into society."[87] Because the Romans deemed Christians a threat to the political order, the political rulers presented them to the populace as spectacle entertainment and had them killed in the

85. Ibid., 337.

86. Surin, *Freedom Not Yet*, 232.

87. Kyle, *Spectacles of Death in Ancient Rome*, 245. See also Tacitus, *Annals*, 15.44.

Coliseum and arenas of the empire. Despite this persecution, Christians viewed the spectacle entertainments as an opportunity to present themselves as disciples of the True Spectacle, whom they knew as the Bread of the World.

Even after the conversion of Constantine, the church maintained its insistence on a mode of conversion that separated Christians from mainstream Roman culture, including spectacle entertainments. For Augustine, conversion was a process of breaking down the catechumen and cleansing him of his malformed desires so that he could be made into the bread of Christ. He told them, "You began to be ground [as grain] by fasts and exorcisms"; with the waters of baptism "you were moistened into dough and made into one lump"; with the fire of the Holy Spirit "you were baked and made into the Lord's loaf of bread."[88] When at last they came to partake of the Eucharist, he directed them to the elements of bread and wine, and said, "there you are on the table, and there you are in the cup . . . it is to what you yourselves are that you say amen."[89] In *City of God*, Augustine engages his pagan interlocutors in order to describe the ways pagan religiosity had degraded Roman civilization and brought it under the influence of demons. Augustine argued that Rome needed to recognize the one true God of Christianity and Christianity's corresponding political ontology, which emerges from the worship of Christ as the True Mediator between divinity and humanity.

In their search for the possibility of a new political ontology, Michael Hardt and Antonio Negri admire the political subjectivity of early Christianity for its capacity to resist effectively the Roman Empire:

> Allow us, in conclusion, one final analogy that refers to the birth of Christianity in Europe and its expansion during the decline of the Roman Empire. In this process an enormous potential of subjectivity was constructed and consolidated in terms of the prophecy of a world to come, a chiliastic project. This new subjectivity offered an absolute alternative to the spirit of imperial right—a new ontological basis. From this perspective, Empire . . . was challenged in its totality by a completely different ethical and ontological axis. In the same way today, given that the limits and unresolvable problems of the new imperial right are fixed, theory and practice can go beyond them, finding once again an ontological basis of

88. Augustine, *Essential Sermons*, 83.

89. Ibid. 284.

antagonism—within Empire, but also against and beyond Empire, at the same level of totality.[90]

Given their admiration for early Christian resistance to Empire, one would expect Marxists like Hardt, Negri, and Surin to see Christianity and its "ontological assets" as an ally in the fight against the new Empire. Hardt and Negri describe the new Empire as "a series of national and supranational organisms united under a single logic of rule."[91] Whereas colonial nation-states maintained their power through strictly managed boundaries of race, geography, language, currency, and cultural tradition, the new mode of Empire, according to Hardt and Negri, thrives on breaking down barriers, is infinitely adaptable, and shapes social life around the mechanisms of consumption and production. However, they insist that despite the relative merits of Christianity, any new political subjectivity must proceed from a purely immanent ontology and must eschew any interest in transcendence. They contrast their vision for a new political subjectivity with Augustine's vision of the City of God, saying,

> there is no God the Father and no transcendence. Instead there is our immanent labor. The teleology of the multitude is theurgical . . . The multitude has no reason to look outside its own history and its own present productive power for the means necessary to lead toward its constitution as a political subject . . . the multitude interprets the telos of an *earthly city*, torn away by the power of its own destiny from any belonging to a *city of God*, which has lost all honor and legitimacy. To the metaphysical and transcendent mediations . . . are thus opposed the absolute constitution of labor and cooperation, the earthly city of the multitude.[92]

Hardt and Negri's vision for a wholly immanent ontology is based in their understanding of two aspects of modernity, one bad and one good.

---

90. Hardt and Negri, *Empire*, 21. Hardt and Negri later write, "we might take inspiration from Saint Augustine's vision of a project to contest the decadent Roman Empire. No limited community could succeed and provide an alternative to imperial rule; only a universal, catholic community bringing together all populations and all languages in a common journey could accomplish this. The divine city is a universal city of aliens, coming together, cooperating, communicating. Our pilgrimage on earth, however, in contrast to Augustine's, has no transcendent telos beyond; it is and remains absolutely immanent. Its continuous movement, gathering aliens in community, making this world its home, is both means and end, or rather a means without an end" (207).

91. Ibid., xii.

92. Ibid., 396. Hardt and Negri's italics.

The good aspect of modernity refers to the "primary event of modernity: the affirmation of the powers of this world, the discovery of the plane of immanence."[93] In the fourteenth century, Duns Scotus told his contemporaries that "the confusion and decadence of the times can be remedied only by re-centering thought on the singularity of being. This singularity is not ephemeral nor accidental but ontological."[94] The effect was a univocity of being whereby human beings began to realize that the powers that had been ascribed "to the heavens" could be attained by human beings: "humanity discovered its power in the world and integrated this dignity into a new consciousness of reason and potentiality."[95] Many philosophers and theologians, such as Nicholas of Cusa and Pico della Mirandola, built upon this ontological foundation to shift from the transcendent plane to the immanent plane where human beings realized themselves as self-originating and self-sustaining: "[T]he powers of creation that had previously been consigned exclusively to the heavens are now brought down to earth. This is the discovery of the fullness of the plane of immanence . . . It develops knowledge and action as scientific experimentation and defines a tendency toward a democratic politics, posing humanity and desire at the center of history."[96] Eventually, in the work of Spinoza, "the horizon of immanence and the horizon of democratic political order coincide completely,"[97] creating the ontological possibility for the multitude to realize its liberation by opposing the metaphysics of the previous era. The multitude is a singularity that worships no one and nothing, and is mediated by no outside force. It works only for itself without the need for transcendence; it sets forth "the splendors of revolutionary humanism, putting humanity and nature in the position of God, transforming the world into a territory of practice, and affirming the democracy of the multitude as the absolute form of politics."[98]

According to Hardt and Negri, the revolution of the immanent plane of being and the possibility of multitude was short-circuited by a counterrevolution that tried to contain the multitude with a metaphysical politics. Although an immanent ontology had been realized apart from any notion of God, modernity invented a "transcendental political apparatus" to

93. Ibid., 71.
94. Ibid.
95. Ibid.
96. Ibid., 73–74.
97. Ibid.
98. Ibid., 77.

mediate subjectivity and functionally replace God. Kantian metaphysics, for example, was "the definitive liquidation of the humanist revolution" because Kant's transcendental argument is the "impossibility of every form of immediacy, the exorcism of every vital figure in the apprehension and action of being."[99] The Kantian subject is a person caught in crisis, "lost in experience, deluded in the pursuit of the ethical ideal."[100] Through Kant's philosophy, modernity's counterrevolution reconnected politics and metaphysics: "[M]odern European metaphysics arose in response to the challenge of the liberated singularities and the revolutionary constitution of the multitude. It functioned as an essential weapon . . . it provided a transcendent apparatus that could impose order on the multitude and prevent it from organizing itself spontaneously and expressing its creativity autonomously . . . the dominant theme was thus to eliminate the medieval form of transcendence that only inhibits production and consumption while maintaining transcendence's effects of domination in a form adequate to the modes of association and production of the new humanity."[101]

Hardt and Negri argue that political theory must throw off the oppression of both modern and premodern metaphysics in order to realize "a material affirmation of liberation" through the political power of immanent labor.[102] "When the multitude works it produces autonomously and reproduces the entire world of life. Producing and reproducing autonomously mean constructing a new ontological reality. In effect, by working, the multitude produces itself as singularity. It is a singularity that establishes a new place in the non-place of Empire, a singularity that is a reality produced by cooperation, represented by the linguistic community, and developed by the movements of hybridization."[103] Thus the multitude as a resistance to Empire differs sharply from the political community of the early church. Whereas early Christian subjectivity was realized in the metaphysical interconnections of the ecclesial, sacramental, and incarnate bodies of Christ, the sheer force of the multitude's life and work in the world holds it together. Early Christians believed that the integrity of their community could only be maintained through the conversion of individual subjects, which involved a reorientation of desire (by exorcism, catechesis,

99. Ibid., 81.
100. Ibid.
101. Ibid., 83.
102. Ibid., 395.
103. Ibid.

and the ritual purification of baptism) and regular communion with God (Eucharist, prayer, worship, spiritual disciplines). Only then could a person be admitted to the community, and only then was he truly free and able to oppose the empire's powers of social production, including spectacle and idolatry.

The fundamental difference between Hardt and Negri, on the one hand, and early Christians like Augustine, on the other, is anthropological: how they understand the question of the human being and its mediation, or lack thereof. For Hardt and Negri, the human subject is ontologically constituted by his labor and is therefore in no need of conversion of desire. He only needs to be freed of metaphysical mediations and distortions of his being so that he can realize himself as an absolute immanent power producing and reproducing his own life. The oppression the subject experiences is always outside himself—it is never a consequence of distorted and misdirected desire—and resistance to oppression is what binds the multivalent multitude into a single political subjectivity. Augustine, on the other hand, addresses both the interior as well as exterior forces at work on the subject. Moreover, for Augustine the question is not *whether* a person will be mediated metaphysically but *which* metaphysics will most fundamentally shape his being.

The weakness of Hardt and Negri's political ontology is that it must deny the innately religious character of the subject. They are right to suggest that Western culture has culminated in a new form of Empire, but this arrival corresponds to a new pagan religiosity and longing for transcendence that cannot simply be denied. Posing pure immanence against humanity's religious nature means they have no way of converting the Consumer Subject—who has been mediated by the glittering but poisoned gifts of demonic metaphysics—except to assert a metaphysical austerity. In other words, his metaphysical sensibilities and religious longing, which have been shaped by consumption as *modus operandi* and by images as *modus significandi*, are not redirected and formed in beneficial ways, but must simply be shut off and altogether denied. It can hardly be true that starving the spirit of the subject by insisting on immanence will produce a better effect than the malnourishment of the spectacle; neither will it ultimately win him over. Rather, what is needed is a means of counteracting the demonic metaphysics of consumerism. The Consumer Subject returns again and again to the idols and metaphysics of the society of the spectacle because consuming does not satiate his desire. Therefore, the goal should not be denying his innate longing for communion with Transcendence, but redirecting him toward the true worship of God.

Like Hardt and Negri, Surin argues that a new political subjectivity can only emerge from an absolute immanent plane. However, he shares some affinity with what I am suggesting to the extent that he seeks to transform the raw energy of consumer culture and the society of the spectacle. He says that the de-transcendentalization of social life in Western democracy has degraded the ontological foundation of the Citizen Subject, but it has also given way to an "uncoded pathos" that drives popular culture and the society of the spectacle. He says that this release of pathos represents "a profoundly missed opportunity" to employ it as a force for liberation that "could have instituted an alternative cultural political regime in which truth and affect would have jointly guided the will linked to *eros*, and thus powerfully politicized."[104] In other words, rather than allow the force of uncoded pathos to feed the production of consumer subjectivity *ad infinitum*, Surin asks if it is possible perhaps to recode this pathos in ways that are liberating. Though he sees potential in this recoding of pathos, he acknowledges that it is unlikely to happen: "we cannot be certain that [it] represents a realistic cultural political option in advanced capitalist societies. To repoliticize what has so far been massively depoliticized will be something akin to a revolutionary undertaking."[105]

Surin is right about the revolutionary nature of redirecting uncoded pathos, but the task is less daunting if we refuse to be held captive to the limits of Scotist univocity and cease from the arbitrary exclusion of theological metaphysics. Early Christianity provides a powerful paradigm for interrupting the symbolic order that has produced social life around the operations of capitalist consumption and production. For early Christianity the pathos of the Coliseum was an opportunity for witness to God and for effectively mobilizing the lower classes and outcasts of Empire, who eventually became the church. On this point, it is helpful to revisit Robin Darling Young's observation that "martyrdom was a spectacle played on the terms of Graeco-Roman society . . . Christian communities invaded those spectacles and turned them to their own purposes . . . they for the first time provided victim-victors who came from the lower classes, or who were women."[106] The Christian martyr was the exemplification of the will

104. Surin, *Freedom Not Yet*, 237.

105. Ibid.

106. Young, *In Procession Before the World*, 12–13.

guided by *eros*, a person whose commitments and desires are so perfectly in accord that they overcome death itself through absolute love for God.

Recovering Exorcism and Renunciation

The early church provided a powerful and effective witness in Rome's society of the spectacle, but what does the church's witness look like in the modern society of the spectacle? Do we have a church that is capable of producing what Hardt and Negri so admire in early Christianity: "a new subjectivity [that] offered an absolute alternative to the spirit of imperial right—a new ontological basis." Can today's church challenge the new mode of Empire "in its totality by a completely different ethical and ontological axis"? Certainly, there are Christians offering such resistance today in the way they live, worship, and witness; but sadly this is not the case for the majority of Christian churches in the West, particularly in the United States.[107]

A recovery of the church's witness can begin with the recognition that our "post-Constantinian" context presents us with many of the challenges that faced Augustine and his contemporaries, because our context is a mirror reflection of Augustine's context. Whereas Augustine wrestled with the society of the spectacle amidst the early *construction* of Christendom, today we wrestle with the society of the spectacle amidst the *deconstruction* of Constantinianism. In Augustine's time, Christianity was officially established, but its values had not taken root in the wider culture in which spectacle entertainments continued to thrive; and today the residue of Christian influence is still visible, but for all intents and purposes, it is culturally disestablished.

In order to compensate for the disestablishment of Christianity, and the rise of the society of the spectacle, many churches in the United States have tended to employ one of two strategies. The first strategy has been to accommodate and acquiesce to the society of the spectacle in the name of relevance and evangelism. For example, many evangelical churches and megachurches—and, increasingly, mainline Protestant churches—have developed models of church life and worship that appeal to worshipers as Consumer Subjects. These churches have sought to evangelize by making church look and feel like entertainment venues; they have replaced

---

107. The "ordinary radical" and "new monastic" movements are examples of contemporary Christians who have renounced the society of the spectacle and conceived a new ontological basis.

traditional pews, stained glass, and steeples with theater seating and screens in order to look and feel more like theaters or sports arenas. They have abandoned the traditional liturgy in favor of worship services that appeal to the sensibilities of the Consumer Subject, and they have developed models of church life and teaching that are easily packaged and marketed. Their members experience the church as consumers of programs that are tailored to their particular interests, age group, and life experience. These programs usually forgo the particularities of denominational traditions and theological distinction because Consumer Subjects do not find such things relevant to their personal lived experience; they distinguish between Lutherans, Methodists, Catholics, and Presbyterians the way they distinguish between Wendy's, McDonald's, Subway, and Burger King. Smith observes that the worshiping lives of many churches are

> a sort of parody of the mall. Rather than properly countering the liturgy of consumption, the church ends up mimicking it, merely substituting Christian commodities—"Jesufied" versions of worldly products, which are acquired, accumulated, and disposed of to make room for the new and the novel. This happens, I think, mainly because we fail to see the practices of consumption as *liturgies*. Typical Christian analysis of the situation, including the critique of materialism (where that still happens), tends to focus on *what* is being purchased, rather than calling into question the *gospel* of consumption—the sense that acquisition brings happiness and fulfillment.[108]

Generally speaking, it is easier for larger churches to incorporate spectacle because doing so is usually very expensive. Nevertheless, churches of every size and type believe that this incorporation of spectacle is a necessary investment. The more a church embraces spectacle, the easier it is to attract Consumer Subjects and keep them involved. One reason for the church's failure to challenge the society of the spectacle is the unprecedented pressure to increase church membership, especially as per capita giving rates decline. Consumer Subjects appraise the relative benefit of the church in light of other entertainment venues, social groups, charity organizations, culture producers, and leisure activities available to them. Pastors who accommodate the society of the spectacle often find themselves in competition with the movie theater and the golf course.

---

108. Smith, *Desiring the Kingdom*, 103. Smith's italics.

The second strategy involves avoiding engagement with the society of the spectacle while clinging to modes of worship and church life that were developed before the church was disestablished. Many mainline Protestant and Catholic churches have adopted this strategy, and they often argue that their modes of worship are more faithful and theologically substantive than those that accommodate the spectacle. In opposition to the society of the spectacle, they proclaim traditional liturgies and aesthetics. They prefer pews and liturgical colors to screens and performance-oriented modes of worship. However, these churches are in decline and their congregations are aging. Their pews are occupied by those who grew up when participation in the church was a *sine qua non* of the wider culture. Their memories stretch back to an era when stores were closed on Sundays and giving to the church was expected. The average age in the PC(USA), for example, is sixty-one, and in 2009 the PC(USA) lost more than sixty-three thousand members, which calculates to roughly 170 members every twenty-four hours.[109]

Churches that follow the second strategy are sometimes invested in liberal theologies that emphasize social justice and tolerance. These are *essential* and *important* values, but they are also widely available in the surrounding culture. Today, values such as tolerance, diversity, pluralism, free critical inquiry, and the authority of human experience are not revolutionary but accepted and commoditized in the society of the spectacle. It is not clear why the torture and death of a first-century Jew and belief in his miraculous resurrection are necessary for espousing these liberal ideals. Of course, theologians and pastors have worked hard to articulate the connections between Christianity and liberalism, but the typical Consumer Subject has no need for such theological substantiation of his beliefs, because consumer culture and liberal democracy provide him with all the rationale and justification he needs to be tolerant and respectful of difference.[110]

---

109. "PC(USA) Congregations and Membership, 1998 to 2009." See http://www.pcusa.org/media/uploads/research/pdfs/2009_table_1.pdf.

110. Christian Smith refers to what he describes as "the cultural triumph of liberal Protestantism." He cites N. Jay Demarath, who says, "Far from representing failure, the decline of Liberal Protestantism may actually stem from its success. It may be the painful structural consequences of [its] wider cultural triumph . . . Liberal Protestants have lost structurally at the micro level precisely because they won culturally at the macro level." To this Smith adds that the values of liberal Protestantism, including "individualism, pluralism, emancipation, tolerance, free critical inquiry, and the authority of human experience," which "have come to so permeate broader American culture that its own churches as organizations have difficulty surviving." Smith, *Souls in Transition*, 287–88.

Augustine and the early church provide us with an alternative to these two strategies. Augustine regarded each subject as a *habitus* of desires and thoughts, which had been corrupted by spectacle but which nevertheless indicated a deep longing for God. Only Christ, who had become a spectacle that he might save the world, could satiate the longing for communion with transcendence indicative in consumption. Augustine and his contemporaries directly addressed this disordered desire and turned the desire for spectacle and consumption toward the mysteries of the sacrament. This turning of desire involved ascetic practices, including ritual exorcism and renunciation. Our contemporary practices do not acknowledge the need for a conversion of desire. As Kenda Creasy Dean observes, "most mainline Protestants do not consider dehabituating practices essential to Christian identity—a position that belies a numbing level of enculturation."[111] If the contemporary church is to challenge the new constitution of Empire as the early church did the Roman Empire, then we must recover an ontological foundation for subjectivity grounded in the Eucharist; but this requires exorcising the consumer subjectivity wrought by the society of the spectacle.

Today we need to recover the fundamental connections between Eucharist, exorcism, and subjectivity. Contemporary theologians such as Catherine Pickstock, Stanley Hauerwas, and Bill Cavanaugh have offered compelling and influential accounts of the Eucharist as the ontological foundation for Christian subjectivity, but the renewal of sacramental theology in theological ethics has yet to recognize the role of exorcism in this equation.[112] In *Torture and Eucharist,* Cavanaugh offers accounts of how the Eucharist provided the ontological basis for Christian subjectivity under the tyrannical government of Chile's Augusto Pinochet in the 1970s and 1980s. Part of the brilliance of Cavanaugh's work in *Torture and Eucharist* is placing the early church's resistance to torture within a modern context. Eucharist became the basis for Chilean Christians' subjectivity under the torturous regime of Pinochet, as it was for early Christians under the persecutions of Rome. Like their predecessors, Chileans connected to Christ's suffering through the Eucharist, and through this identification they embodied the link between the ecclesial body of Christ and the sacramental body of Christ. Cavanaugh's work is a watershed in theological ethics in part because it provides a concrete example of the relationship between

111. Dean, *Practicing Passion*, 205.

112. See, for example, Cavanaugh, *Torture and Eucharist*; Pickstock, *After Writing*; and Hauerwas, *The Hauerwas Reader*.

Eucharist and subjectivity. However, his insights do not easily translate to Western consumer culture where Christianity is not persecuted. Whereas torture in Chile was an overt means of coercion centered in government authority, the society of the spectacle is a covert and decentralized oppression that gains control through the processes of consumption and production. The Consumer Subject does not experience it as oppression because it dovetails with the values of liberal democracy, particularly freedom and individual autonomy. His consumption and insatiable desire are not taken as signs of oppression but as expressions of his personal preferences and individuality. Whereas torture oppresses through brute force, the society of the spectacle is like a parasite that finds a host in both the individual subject and social life. Dislodging this parasite is the function of exorcism. Only when the subject is free from his malformed desires can he come to desire the goodness, truth, and beauty made available to him in the Eucharist. Thus, sacramental theology and theological ethics must recover the relationship between exorcism and Eucharist, because the efficacy of the Eucharist as the ontological basis of subjectivity requires exorcising the demons that have corrupted the desires of the subject through the various expressions and mechanisms of the society of the spectacle (consumerism, marketing, entertainment, and so forth).

In *Desiring the Kingdom*, James K. A. Smith says that "baptism is a moment when Christian worship articulates an antithesis with respect to the world" because Christians should be "a called-out people who are marked as strange because they are a community that desires the kingdom of God."[113] Smith further suggests that maintaining this disposition of "the cruciform shape exemplified in Christ" requires "a series of renunciations or even exorcisms that renounce Satan and the world."[114] Although such renunciations have, for the most part, disappeared from much of Western Christianity, they have been handed down to us in the Episcopal Book of Common Prayer. They come in the form of questions and answers on Satan, transcendent evil power, and desire that are posed to the Christian at the moment of baptism:

> Do you renounce Satan and all the spiritual forces of wickedness that rebel against God?
>
> *I renounce them.*

113. Smith, *Desiring the Kingdom*, 187.
114. Ibid.

Do you renounce the evil powers of this world, which corrupt and destroy the creatures of God?

I renounce them.

Do you renounce all sinful desires that draw you from the love of God?

I renounce them.

Do you turn to Jesus Christ and accept him as your savior?

I do.

Do you put your whole trust in his grace and love?

I do.

Do you promise to follow and obey him as your Lord?

I do.[115]

Smith contends that these renunciations of Satan and evil, and affirmations of love for Christ as savior and Lord, "are to be ongoing . . . not a singular event but a way of life . . . Our baptism signals that we are new creatures, with new desires, a new passion for a very different kingdom; thus we renounce (and keep renouncing) our former desires."[116]

In our secularized world, the notions of ritual exorcism and renunciation evoke a sense of superstition and suspicion, but these practices need not feel any more foreign than a Call to Confession, which is still a regular and familiar part of the liturgy in many congregations. Whereas confession focuses on admission of personal and corporate sin, renunciation involves formally identifying the cultural and institutional manifestations of spiritual powers. Thus, Smith suggests that renunciation is practical and pertains to concrete questions of how the "cultural practices and institutions are bent on forming in you 'sinful desires that draw you from the love of God.'"[117] He advises thinking about "the particular configurations of cultural institutions and practices that need to be (daily!) renounced in order to truly foster human flourishing . . . Consider using them as aids for

---

115. *Book of Common Prayer*, cited in Smith, *Desiring the Kingdom*, 186.

116. Ibid., 188–89.

117. Ibid.

meditation before receiving communion."[118] Whereas renunciation can be personal and function as a meditation aid before communion, exorcism is innately corporate. It is the acknowledgment that, without the power of Christ, we cannot renounce the powers that occupy our heart, mind, and spirit. We need the Holy Spirit to remove these powers, and we need the support of the body of Christ to be filled anew with the goodness of the gospel. The powers that come to occupy us are diverse. What one person struggles with another may find benign. Being in an accountable community helps us realize that where one person is weak another may be strong, and we can help one another overcome our vulnerabilities and temptations. For example, the Apostle Paul wrote to the Corinthians regarding meat sacrificed to idols (1 Cor 8). Some in the Corinthian community experienced eating this meat as a doorway of the demonic, while for others it was simply meat. Paul acknowledged and affirmed both perspectives: "We are no worse off if we do not eat, and no better off if we do" (1 Cor 8:8). However, he counseled the stronger members of the Corinthian community to refrain for the sake of their sisters and brothers, saying, "Be careful that the exercise of your freedom does not become a stumbling block to the weak . . . If what I eat causes my brother to fall into sin, I will never eat meat again, so that I will not cause him to fall" (1 Cor 8:9, 13).

To renounce Satan and evil "as a way of life" is to live into a metaphysical worldview that recognizes that evil exceeds the immanent plane of being. In other words, evil as we experience it is not merely a matter of human sinfulness and will. As William Desmond observes, "Evil sometimes seems unloosed with a life of its own, outside our best good will and power. It seems to have a power disproportionate to anything attributable to the evil we undoubtedly originate."[119] Moreover, "Even if we make some sense of moral evil by attribution to our will, the issue is evil relative to creation, not just the human creature. Does the story of the Fall name the malignancy, the sometimes demonic energies unloosed, energies other to human will? There seems evil in excess of the moral evil we can impute to any human agent. Do we invoke a more than human agency? There seems no a priori reason to rule this out."[120] To speak of the transcendence of Satan and evil is not the same as arguing for radical evil, which ascribes ontology to evil itself. Rather, it is to recognize, as Augustine and his contemporaries did,

---

118. Ibid, 189.

119. Desmond, *God and the Between*, 331.

120. Ibid., 257.

that human beings are open to good and bad influences from beyond; in Desmond's words we are porous to influences that transcend us, whether good or bad. Augustine regarded evil as privation, but he also recognized that rebellion against God is not confined to the immanent plane of being. He regarded Satan as a fallen creature who in his rebellion maintains his creaturely status. His only power is to pervert and distort what is good. Augustine said, "[T]he Devil was once without sin . . . sin first came into existence as a result of the Devil's pride . . . the Devil is the Lord's handiwork. For there is nothing in nature, even among the last and least of the little creatures, which is not brought into being by [God], from whom comes all form, all shape, all order; and without those definitions nothing can be found in nature or imagined in the mind. How much more must the angelic creation derive from him."[121]

A humility comes with the realization that rebellion against God does not originate with us. The rebel does not achieve independence from the Creator but merely becomes an imitator of the demonic; he is not self-determinate but merely seduced and corrupted by Satan. This is why the modern rebellion against God needed to dispense with *both* God and Satan. Russian novelist Fyodor Dostoyevsky illustrated this in his masterpiece, *The Brothers Karamazov*. The novel examines the lives of three brothers, but I want to focus on the relationship between two of them, Alyosha and Ivan, who represent two very different worldviews. Alyosha, the younger brother, is a monk with a deep soul and profound compassion, and his mentor, the Elder Zosima, sends him away from the monastery to minister in the world. As Alyosha leaves, Zosima says, "You are more needed there. There is no peace there. You will serve and be of use. If demons raise their heads, recite a prayer."[122] Soon after his departure, Alyosha encounters Ivan, who shares none of his spiritual and metaphysical sensibilities. Ivan is a modern rationalist with no time for naïve belief in God. He admonishes Alyosha: "You see, my dear, there was in the eighteenth century an old sinner who stated that if God did not exist he would have to be invented. And man has indeed invented God . . . I think that if the Devil does not exist, and man has therefore created him, he has created him in his own image and likeness."[123] Ivan conflates God and the Devil and renders them as two aspects of the same problem, which is belief in transcendence. His method

121. Augustine, *City of God* 11.15 (Bettenson, 447).

122. Dostoyevsky, *Brothers Karamazov*, 77.

123. Ibid., 239.

reflects the modern notion that speaking of God, the Devil, or anything beyond immanent reality is merely the projection of human imagination onto concepts that exist only in the mind. *God* refers to the better part of human nature, while *Devil* signifies the human propensity for evil. Yet for all of his skepticism and rationalism, Ivan is overcome by the Devil. In the penultimate chapter of *The Brothers Karamazov*, the Devil visits him in a vision. Ivan says, "Not for a single moment do I take you for the real truth . . . You are the embodiment of myself, but of just one side of me . . . of my thoughts and feelings, but only the most loathsome and stupid of them."[124] However, the more Ivan asserts his modern rationalism against the Devil, the more he falls into the Devil's grip. In his growing desperation Ivan proclaims, "You want to overcome me with realism, to convince me that you are, but I don't want to believe that you are! I won't believe!" The Devil then replies calmly, "But I'm not lying, its all true; unfortunately the truth is hardly ever witty." When his vision finally ends and the Devil disappears, Ivan exclaims to himself, "That was no dream! No, I swear it was no dream, it all just happened!"[125]

Ivan's story is the story of modernity. Modernity attempted a rational rebellion against God by denying transcendence. In the wake of the Enlightenment, God and the Devil were rendered objects of the mind. Yet this rebellion has failed and in reality the Devil's grip has tightened. Today, humanity has abandoned the pretensions of rational modernity and gone out in search of genuine Transcendence, which it tries to find in the false transcendences and seductions of the market's demonic metaphysics. In Dostoyevsky's novel, Ivan is released from the Devil's torments only by the arrival of Alyosha. Ivan exclaims, "He [the Devil] got frightened of you [Alyosha], of you, a dove. You're a pure cherub . . . The thundering shout of the seraphim's rapture!"[126] We require a holy presence to chase away the Devil's torments and release us from captivity to our disordered desires. In the days of Rome, such disruption was the powerful witness of Christian martyrs.

Today's Living Martyrs

In his first letter to the Corinthians, the Apostle Paul wrote, "For it seems to me that God has put us apostles on display at the end of the procession, like

124. Ibid., 637.
125. Ibid., 650.
126. Ibid., 651.

men condemned to die in the arena. We have been made a spectacle to the whole universe, to angels as well as to men" (1 Cor 4:9 NIV). These words describe the lived experience of early Christian martyrs who were led into the Coliseum and amphitheaters of the empire to become spectacles for the world. For Ignatius of Antioch, martyrdom was an opportunity to follow in the footsteps of Christ. Like Jesus of Nazareth, he willingly accepted his martyrdom and turned the society of the spectacle on its head by testifying to the body and blood of Christ as the true spectacle. Martyrdom was a powerful witness in Rome's society of the spectacle, but what do martyrdom and witness look like today in the modern society of the spectacle?

If we conceive of martyrdom not as death but as the capacity of the Christian to interrupt Empire's symbolic order through renunciation of the spectacle and of consumption, then it becomes possible to speak of living martyrs. This is not to diminish the significance of actual martyrdom but to highlight what it means to be "dead to the world" and "alive to Christ." One example of living martyrs thriving and witnessing in our modern society of the spectacle are the new monastics and other intentional Christian communities whose lives *interrupt the symbolic order* of the spectacle with vows of simplicity and community. Like their early Christian predecessors, they are not extraordinary individuals but ordinary radicals whose lives correspond to an alternative ontology made possible by the life, death, and resurrection of Christ and by the gift of the Eucharist. The sacrificial nature of their vows of simplicity stands in stark contrast to the pleasures and excesses of consumer subjectivity. However, they do not live austere lives of solitude, as some of their monastic precursors once did, but instead choose to live fully in the world. Of course, the pleasures of consumer subjectivity are as available to them as to anyone else in Western culture, but their desires are informed by a different metaphysical reality. Daily they renounce the society of the spectacle, and they seek to be thoroughly mediated not by demonic metaphysics but by the metaphysical possibilities of salvation professed by the Christian faith. Their witness counters the seduction of spectacle with the "irresistible revolution" of "the simple way."[127] We need to pay special attention to the simple way of these examples of living martyrs, for they provide us with a concrete and powerful example of what it means to witness in the modern society of the spectacle.

127. See Claiborne, *The Irresistible Revolution*.

4

Ecstasy, Spectacle, and Consumption

There is no spectacle without disturbance to the spirit . . . For even if a
man enjoys spectacles modestly and uprightly, as befits his status or age
or even his natural disposition, his soul is not unstirred and he is not
without a silent rousing of the spirit.

—TERTULLIAN, *ON SPECTACLES*, 15.3, 5

The last chapter argued that metaphysics is alive and well in the modern
society of the spectacle despite the postmetaphysical suppositions of contemporary political theory and philosophy. It described how the society of
the spectacle portrays heaven as a realm of infinite desire, a transcendent
paradise free of material limitations where perfect and immortal bodies
can consume without limit. Augustine described this false paradise as
the realm of the demons, a liminal space between transcendence and immanence where immortality and the passions of the soul sing in concert.
The previous chapter also contrasted the society of the spectacle and the
church by seeing them as different modes of consumption that correspond
to different metaphysical mediations. It showed that, whereas the church is
a society that cultivates deep satisfaction through the consumption of the
Eucharist, the society of the spectacle reflects the insatiable desire proper
to the demons.

This chapter further juxtaposes the church and the society of the
spectacle as different modes of consumption by contrasting the role ecstasy
plays in each. Although ecstasy is not a theological concept that receives

much attention in modern theology, it played an important role in the theology of Thomas Aquinas, and, as we shall see, it plays an important role in the metaphysical mediations of the society of the spectacle. For Thomas, ecstasy refers to the experience of being drawn out of oneself by love for another. It names an experience of being severed from an old self in order to be transformed into a new self through unification with the beloved. Eucharist is the quintessential example of ecstasy, because the lover of Christ is drawn out of his old, sinful self and into a deeper unity with Him. Aquinas says that as the lover of Christ is drawn out of himself, he experiences a "suffering," because he is being severed from his old self. His old self is "pierced" and "melted" in order to be transformed and unified with Christ. However, this suffering is temporary and ultimately leads to the "perfection of the lover," which means that the lover "is centered on the beloved and living with and for the other rather than turned in upon himself and living for himself alone."[1]

For Thomas it is significant that this ecstatic unification of the lover and Christ comes through an act of consumption. Aquinas observes that the Eucharist is directly connected to our bodily sustenance, and he compares the consumption of the "spiritual food" of the Eucharist with the nourishment that comes with consuming ordinary food. While ordinary consumption involves a transformation of food into the body of the consumer (i.e., the food becomes part of the body), consuming the spiritual food of the Eucharist transforms the consumer into the body of Christ. As Peter Kwasniewski observes, for Thomas, the "spiritual food" of the Eucharist "is not converted into the one eating; the one eating is rather converted into it, for it acts upon him so as to turn him into itself."[2] Just as we must take food into ourselves regularly to maintain health and strength, so too must we consume Christ regularly to be continually nourished by him; this nourishment unifies us with him. Our continual need for consuming the Eucharist is an ongoing reminder of our status as finite beings who are dependent on God for our very existence. The Eucharist cultivates a sense of gratitude and a perspective that regards the world and all its resources as a gift.

In this chapter, eucharistic ecstasy will provide a vantage point from which to understand the ecstasies cultivated in consumers by the society of the spectacle. These ecstasies are carefully designed to cultivate a person's lower appetites and to make him a prisoner of them. They are what Aquinas

1. Kwasniewski, "Ecstasy of Love in Aquinas's *Commentary on the Sentences*," 61.
2. Kwasniewski, "St. Thomas on Eucharistic Ecstasy," 165.

calls "debasing ecstasy," and they are a distortion of the good or "intellective ecstasy" exemplified in the Eucharist. The debasing ecstasies of the society of the spectacle are a simulacra of eucharistic ecstasy, which satisfies the soul and replenishes the spirit through communion with God. Moreover, Aquinas observes that in addition to satisfying the soul, consuming the eucharistic ecstasy effects a deification of the worshiper, for in taking the *sacramental* body of Christ into himself, the worshiper is unified with the *incarnate* body of Christ according to an analogical metaphysics (*analogia entis*). Because this unification comes through ecstasy, Aquinas describes it as "inebriation." He says, "This is a food [i.e., Eucharist] capable of making man divine and inebriating him with divinity,"[3] and again, "This cup is the gift of divine love which inebriates, since one who is drunk is not in himself . . . for he is made *to be in ecstasy* . . . .the cup means the blood of Christ which ought to make us drunk."[4] Whereas eucharistic ecstasy "inebriates with divinity," the ecstasies of the society of the spectacle leave consumers in the drunken state of perpetual and insatiable desire proper to the demonic.

Ultimately, this chapter's juxtaposition of eucharistic ecstasy to the society of the spectacle transgresses the boundary separating the theological from the secular. For many decades (post)modernity has invested heavily in this boundary in order to secure the autonomy of the secular as distinct from the theological. However, in recent years, those philosophers and theologians associated with Radical Orthodoxy have worked to deconstruct this secure boundary as they have sought to "reclaim the world by situating its concerns and activities within a theological framework."[5] This perspective dovetails with the perspective of this chapter (and of this book as a whole) in that here we seek to articulate the society of the spectacle *not* as a manifestation of secularism but as a metaphysical and theological phenomenon. It is from this postsecular standpoint that this chapter seeks to reclaim consumption from the society of the spectacle by conceiving the Eucharist as the overacceptance of spectacle and debasing ecstasy. By overacceptance, we mean the way the Eucharist signifies the violent spec-

3. Aquinas, *Super Ioan* 6, lec 7, 969, cited in Kwasniewski, "St. Thomas on Eucharistic Ecstasy," 166.

4. Aquinas, Commentary on Psalm 22, cited in Kwasniewski, "St. Thomas on Eucharistic Ecstasy," 166 n. 59. My italics.

5. Reclaiming the world through a theological framework is the stated purpose and intent of scholars working from the position of Radical Orthodoxy. See Milbank, Ward, and Pickstock, "Introduction: Suspending the Material."

tacle of Christ's death as the source of human salvation.[6] This signification renders both spectacle and debasing ecstasy as misdirected desire for God. From this perspective, we will consider the modern society of the spectacle and the ecstasies it produces in consumers. We will also explore how this misdirection can be overaccepted and turned toward the *ecstasy* of Christ's forgiveness. As we will see through the theology of Aquinas and John Milbank, Christ's words of forgiveness ("Father, forgive them; for they know not what they do") pertain to an ecstasy, because they tell of Christ's utter abandonment of himself for the sake of his beloved (i.e., humanity). Moreover, Christ's words of forgiveness relate to ecstasy because they are part of the transformation of the lover (i.e., Christ's resurrection) and his unification with his beloved (through the Eucharist). Through suffering ecstasy Christ achieved an ontological shift that restored humanity and made it possible for humanity to be unified with God.

The rest of this chapter will proceed as follows: after exploring the role of ecstasy in the works of Aquinas, we will use his insights to illuminate Rome's violent spectacles as the production of debasing ecstasy, and we will see how Christ's crucifixion is an overacceptance of this ecstasy. We will then turn to our own context of mass consumer capitalism to see how Aquinas's account of ecstasy illuminates the role ecstasy plays in the modern society of the spectacle. Ecstasy plays an important role in many spectacles: at the shopping mall, in movies, video games, virtual reality, marketing, and so forth. It is not possible to investigate all of these manifestations in detail, so we will look at one particularly important instance: the music festival. Today's music festivals and rock/pop concerts are grand spectacle entertainments, and by interpreting them through a theological metaphysics, we will reveal them as quintessential examples of how the society of the spectacle cultivates ecstasy as a deep longing for Transcendence. This metaphysical analysis of popular music will show how this particular manifestation of the society of the spectacle is not a secular phenomenon (as is generally assumed) but in fact operates a quasi-incarnational metaphysics and even an experience of the *analogia entis*.

---

6. I am indebted to Samuel Wells for my use of "overacceptance." Wells says, "The church does not simply accept the story of evil. It has a story of its own. The church's story begins before evil began and ends after evil has ended. As we shall see, this story does not accept evil—it overaccepts it" (*Improvisation*, 113).

Ecstasy and Eucharist in Aquinas

Aquinas's discussions of ecstasy often appear as part of his writing on other subjects. For example, in Book III, Distinction 27 of the *Sentences*, Aquinas seeks to define love by turning to chapter 4 of Dionysius's *On the Divine Names*, and he notes that for Dionysius, "Love is a unitive and concretive power." Despite his own confidence in Dionysius, Aquinas nevertheless notes nine objections that can be proffered against this notion of love. As Kwasniewski observes, the fourth objection is the longest, and it is particularly striking because it suggests that we experience love *not* as a unifying force but as a dividing force. The fourth objection reads,

> In *On the Heavenly Hierarchies* Dionysius sets down "piercing" [*actum*] and "burning" [*fervidum*] among the properties of love, and "melting," too, is set down as love's effect, as in the Song of Songs: "My soul melted when my beloved spoke" (5:6). In chapter 4 of *On the Divine Names*, Dionysius also sets down "ecstasy," i.e., being placed outside oneself, as love's effect. But all these things seem to pertain to division. The piercing is what divides by penetrating; the burning, what dissolves by exhalations. Melting, too, is a kind of division opposed to freezing. And that which is placed outside itself is divided from itself. Therefore love is more a divisive force than a unitive one.[7]

For Aquinas this objection raises an important question: if ecstatic love is essentially divisive, then how can love and ecstasy coexist?

Aquinas clearly considers this an important question, and he provides a thorough and extensive reply. He acknowledges that in its highest and most powerful form, love does indeed cause the lover to suffer ecstasy, which involves a sense of coming apart, which in turn can be described as penetration, burning, and melting. Moreover, he acknowledges that all of these imply not a unitive but a divisive effect in the lover. However, Aquinas does not see this state of ecstatic suffering as the end of love. Rather, he understands this suffering as the perfecting of love in the lover. Ecstasy does not describe the permanent condition of a person who is in love but the experiences of a person who is in the process of being drawn out and transformed by love. The ecstatic phase of love is an *exitus a se* that "involves an alienation from what has been in order to become, literally, altered."[8] In the

---

7. Aquinas, *Sentences* III. 27.1, quoted in Kwasniewski, "Ecstasy of Love in Aquinas's *Commentary on the Sentences*," 55.

8. Kwasniewski, "St. Thomas Aquinas on Eucharistic Ecstasy," 155.

Summa Aquinas says, "ecstasy means simply going outside oneself by being placed outside one's proper order."[9] Thus, Aquinas understands ecstasy as part of the *process* of dividing the lover from his former self in order to be united with the beloved and thereby transformed. The experience of ecstasy is the dissolution of one's former disposition, and it prepares the way to the unification that love engenders.

Aquinas goes into great detail about the nature of ecstatic love as a dividing force,[10] and Kwasnewski says that he does this in order to emphasize "that love really *transforms* the lover—how, in words inspired by Dionysius, it pierces him, wounds him, sets him aflame, places him out of himself, frees him from limits, melts him . . . in order to make him a perfect lover, centered on the beloved and living with and for the other rather than turned in upon himself and living for himself alone."[11] Aquinas follows Dionysius in identifying the Apostle Paul as a quintessential example of a person transformed by ecstasy. Aquinas says, "Hence man may become outside himself [i.e., ecstasy] . . . when a man's intellective appetite tends wholly to divine things, and takes no account of those things whereto the

9. Aquinas, *Summa*, 2.1, Q. 28, Art 3, New Advent, online.

10. Aquinas discusses the threefold division as part of his reply to the fourth objection quoted above. Kwasnieski helpfully identifies the transitions in Aquinas's text with brackets: "To the fourth, it should be said that in love there is a union of lover and beloved, but there is also a threefold division. [First division:] For by the fact that love transforms the lover into the beloved, it makes the lover enter into the interior of the beloved and vice versa, so that nothing of the beloved remains not united to the lover, just as a form reaches to the inner most recesses of that which it informs and vice versa. Thus the lover in a way penetrates into the beloved and so love is called 'piercing'; for to come into the innermost recesses of a thing by dividing it is characteristic of something piercing. In the same way does the beloved penetrate the lover, reaching to his innermost recesses, and that is why it is said that love 'wounds,' and that it 'transfixes the innards.' [Second division:] But because nothing can be transformed into another without withdrawing, in a way, from its own form, since of a single thing there is a single form, therefore preceding this division of penetration is another division by which the lover, in tending toward the beloved, is separated from himself. And according to this, love is said to bring about ecstasy and to burn, since that which burns rises beyond itself and vanishes into smoke. [Third division:] Further still, because nothing withdraws from itself unless freed from what was containing it within itself, as a natural thing does not lose its form unless the dispositions retaining this form in the matter are unbound, it is therefore necessary that that boundedness by which the lover was contained within his own bounds be taken away from him. And that is why love is said to 'melt the heart,' for a liquid is not contained by its own limits, while the contrary disposition is called 'hardness of heart.'" See Kwasniewski, "Ecstasy of Love in Aquinas's *Commentary on the Sentences*," 59–61.

11. Kwasniewski, "Ecstasy of Love in Aquinas's *Commentary on the Sentences*," 60–61.

sensitive appetite inclines him; thus Dionysius says (*Div. Nom.* iv) that 'Paul being in ecstasy through the vehemence of Divine love' exclaimed: 'I live, now not I, but Christ lives in me.'"[12]

Aquinas notes that someone might object to his description of ecstatic love by pointing out that if love necessarily involves ecstasy, and if ecstasy involves being severed from one's former self, then how is it possible for God to love, since God is impassible and therefore cannot experience the dissolution of the self involved in ecstasy? This objection is compounded by the observation that God is also immutable and thus by God's nature cannot undergo the transformation that ecstasy requires.

Aquinas proffers a reply by first acknowledging the legitimacy of the objection, saying, "Love bears the lover into the beloved, so that he now lives the life of the beloved, as Dionysius says. But God is not borne into anything other, since he is immovable, but rather he draws all things to himself, as is said in John 12."[13] However, he observes that while human beings do indeed experience ecstasy as dissolution of the self, this dissolution happens through the lover realizing that he is not whole, or complete, in himself. Thus, for a human being, the unity that comes through ecstatic love involves a gaining or adding to the life of the lover even as he is emptied of himself and becomes focused on his beloved. Although we benefit in this way from love, God, by virtue of being whole and complete, loves ecstatically, not through the unity that comes from transformation of the self, but by the unity that comes through the outpouring of God's perfect self into the beloved. God loves in excess of God's self, and thus there is an ecstatic going out from Godself for the sake (only) of the creature in a way that does not add to or change God. Whereas humanity loves by participating in the life of the beloved, God loves by communicating goodness to the creature. Aquinas writes, "Granting that the lover always bears the lover into the beloved, Thomas distinguishes two ways in which this can happen. Either the lover is borne into the beloved in the sense of going beyond his limited self to share something that belongs to the beloved [i.e., human love for God], or the lover shares with the beloved something which is already his own [i.e., God's love for humanity]. In both cases the lover is ecstatic."[14] Thus, the contrast between human love for God and divine love for human-

12. Aquinas, *Summa* 2.2, Q 175, Art 2, New Advent online.

13. Aquinas, *Sentences* III.32.1 Obj. 3, cited in Kwasniewski "Ecstasy of Love in Aquinas's *Commentary on the Sentences*," 77.

14. Kwaniewski "Ecstasy of Love in Aquinas's *Commentary on the Sentences*," 82.

ity pertains to receiving versus communicating perfection. In this regard Aquinas says, "God communicates God's goodness to [the creature], and thus Dionysius says that God himself suffers *extasis* through love."[15] This suffering can *only be meant in a metaphorical way*, as when God is said to be angry or sorrowful in Scripture.

The *extasis* of God for the creature underscores that the Creator and the creature are not ontologically univocal. As finite beings we are capable of approximating the love of God, but even our deepest love is but a mere reflection of the way God loves out of God's completeness, perfection, and excessive goodness. That human love is a reflection of God's love underscores the analogical ontology (*analogia entis*) whereby human beings are made in the image of God and reflect God's being. As creatures human beings participate in the infinite goodness that is God, and as Kwasniewski observes, God's ecstasy highlights the way finite humanity draws its being from God's being metaphysically. He notes, "Thomas's understanding of the divine *extasis* thus leads us back to the metaphysics of *esse*—of participation of any finite being, with its act-potency structure and the ecstatic neediness and longing flowing from it, in the perfectly simple, all-sufficient, self-subsistent, infinite act of being which, as giver and sustainer of being to all and in all, is more intimately present to each and every thing than any thing to itself."[16]

For Aquinas, consuming Eucharist is the exemplary way in which finite humanity participates in God, and this participation deifies the believer because, as we have noted, the spiritual food of Eucharist transforms us into Christ. As A. N. Williams observes, "Aquinas designates the Eucharist, the preeminent sacrament of Christ's sacrifice, as deifying because its very reality is charity, with respect to both its habit and its act, which the Eucharist 'kindles.'"[17] This kindling of divinity is not merely conceptual but refers to a transformation of the worshiper akin to becoming drunk with ecstasy. Of the Eucharist, Thomas says, "This is a food capable of making man divine and inebriating him with divinity,"[18] and "This cup is the gift of divine love which inebriates, since one who is drunk is not in himself

---

15. Aquinas, *Sentences* III.32.1 ad 3, cited in Kwasniewski "Ecstasy of Love in Aquinas's *Commentary on the Sentences*," 78.

16. Kwasniewski "Ecstasy of Love in Aquinas's *Commentary on the Sentences*," 83.

17. Williams, *Ground of Union*, 93.

18. Aquinas, *Super Ioan* 6, lec 7, 969 , cited in Kwasniewski, "St. Thomas on Eucharistic Ecstasy," 166.

. . . for he is made *to be in ecstasy* . . . .the cup means the blood of Christ which ought to make us drunk."[19] Of course, Aquinas is not advocating literal drunkenness, for he is speaking metaphorically of the transformation effected when a believer consumes the Eucharist. Eucharist leaves a person inebriated, in the sense that it produces an ecstasy, or an experience of having one's constitution melted. Through this inebriation, we are joined to Christ and made (analogical) participants in God's happiness. Thomas says, "God is happiness by his essence: for he is happy not by acquisition or participation of something else, but by his essence. On the other hand, men are happy, as Boëthius says, by participation; just as they are called *gods,* by participation. And this participation of happiness, in respect of which man is said to be happy, is something created."[20] Ultimately, Aquinas provides us with a conceptual matrix where happiness, love, ecstasy, deification, and Eucharist are all interrelated. These elements work together to enable our analogical participation in God's *esse,* which is in turn a reflection of God's ecstatic love for creation.

In order to understand fully the relations of ecstasy and love to Eucharist and deification, we must grasp what Aquinas means when he says that ecstasy is an "appetitive power." In Aquinas's philosophy of mind, "Absolutely every form has some sort of tendency or inclination."[21] Trees, for example, have an inclination to grow upwards, and "on the basis of its form, fire, for instance, is inclined toward a higher place, and toward generating its like."[22] Inclination is for Aquinas the genus of appetite, and human beings possess in common with animals *sensory* appetites (urges, drives, emotions, etc.), and *irascible* appetites (e.g., the disposition of fleeing what is harmful and overcoming whatever might deter one from what is good for ones' self). Human beings are unique in exercising reason over appetites, but reason's power over the appetites is not always effective. A person's incomplete power over his appetite can be understood in contrast to a person's total power over his body; whereas a normal and healthy person's limbs are always under his control, a person's appetites can control him. Thus, Aquinas describes the relationship between the appetites and reason

19. Aquinas, Commentary on Psalm 22, cited in Kwasniewski, "St. Thomas on Eucharistic Ecstasy," n. 59, 166

20. Aquinas, *Summa* I-II.3 ad 1, cited in Williams, *Ground of Union,* 95.

21. Kretzmann, "Philosophy of Mind," 144.

22. Aquinas, *Summa Theologiae* 1.80.1.c, cited in Kretzmann, "Philosophy of Mind," 144.

as "political," by which he means that the appetites can challenge reason's rightful place of authority in our being: "That is why we experience the irascible or the concupiscible [sensory] appetites fighting against reason when we sense or imagine something pleasant that reason forbids, or something unpleasant that reason commands."[23]

The fragility of the relationship of reason over appetite is significant for how Aquinas thinks about ecstasy. When a person's reason maintains its rightful place of control, he can suffer ecstasy in a positive way, or "as to the apprehensive power." If, on the other hand, a person's appetites overcome him, then he will be "cast down into a state of debasement." Aquinas says,

> I answer that to suffer ecstasy is to be placed outside oneself. This happens as to the apprehensive power and as to the appetive power. As to the apprehensive power, a man is said to be placed outside himself, when he is placed outside the knowledge proper to him. This may be due to his being raised to a higher knowledge; thus, a man is said to suffer ecstasy, inasmuch as he is placed outside the connatural apprehension of his sense and reason, when he is raised up so as to comprehend things that surpass sense and reason.[24]

It is important to recognize that for Aquinas knowledge and ecstasy are not mutually exclusive but can reinforce one another. In Question 175 of the *Summa*, Aquinas uses somewhat different language to describe the juxtaposition of apprehensive power and appetitive power and their respective relation to ecstasy. Here he describes how the "intellective appetite" and the "sensual/lower appetite" can move a person toward either a good or bad ecstasy:

> There is a twofold appetite in man; to wit, the intellective appetite, which is called the will, and the sensitive appetite known as the sensuality. Now it is proper to man that his lower appetite be subject to the higher appetite, and that the higher move the lower. Hence man may become outside himself as regards the appetite, in two ways. In one way, when a man's intellective appetite tends wholly to divine things, and takes no account of those things whereto the sensitive appetite inclines him; thus Dionysius says (*Div. Nom.* iv) that "Paul being in ecstasy through the vehemence of divine love" exclaimed: "I live, now not I, but Christ lives in me."

23. Aquinas, *Summa Theologiae*, 1.81.3, ad 2, cited in Kretzmann, "Philosophy of Mind," 146.

24. Aquinas, *Summa*, 1.1 Q. 28, Art. 3.

In another way, when a man tends wholly to things pertaining to the lower appetite, and takes no account of his higher appetite. It is thus that "he [the prodigal son] who fed the swine debased himself"; and this latter kind of going out of oneself, or being beside oneself [i.e., ecstasy], is more akin than the former to the nature of rapture because the higher appetite is more proper to man. Hence when through the violence of his lower appetite a man is withdrawn from the movement of his higher appetite, it is more a case of being withdrawn from that which is proper to him.[25]

The two kinds of ecstasy (i.e., debasing and intellective) that Aquinas identifies in this passage must further be understood in light of his understanding of the appetitive power as always—without exception—driving us toward "the last end." In other words, as the expression and overflow of God's complete and perfect *esse*, human desire points back to its originating source. Thus, even debasing ecstasy indicates a desire for God (albeit in a misdirected way) and indicates human longing for communion with Transcendence. Aquinas says, "Man must, of necessity, desire all, whatsoever he desires, of the last end . . . First, because whatever man desires, he desires it under the aspect of good. And if he desire it, not as his perfect good, which is the last end, he must, of necessity, desire it as tending to the perfect good, because the beginning of anything is always ordained to its completion."[26]

Thomas's account of debasing ecstasy as indicating a misdirected desire for God opens a new way of understanding Rome's spectacle entertainments and Christ's crucifixion. From this vantage point we can go back to see how spectacle entertainments produced a debasing ecstasy in people such as Augustine and Seneca, who provide firsthand accounts of what it was like to experience the suffering of the spectator. Moreover, we can interpret the spectators at Golgotha as suffering a debasing ecstasy as they participated in the breaking of Christ's body and pouring out of his blood. Through the sacramental logic of the Eucharist, Christ overaccepts this debasing ecstasy and thereby sees in it a longing for God. Though the spectators are not aware of this longing as they gaze up at his cross, Christ is aware of it, and utters words of forgiveness: "Father, forgive them; for they know not what they do." As we shall see in the next section, these

25. Aquinas, *Summa* 2.2 Q 175, Art 2, New Advent online

26. Aquinas, *Summa* I-II, 1, cited in Williams, *Ground of Union*, 94. In this same section Aquinas describes the relation between desire and God in terms of the appetitive power. He says, "The last end stands in the same relation in moving the appetite, as the first mover in other movements."

words of forgiveness are an ecstasy of love that proceeds out of Christ's wholeness, perfection, and completeness. Moreover, this ecstasy is of the "intellective" kind because it pertains to a higher knowledge; Christ knows what the spectators want and need (i.e., forgiveness) even before they know it themselves.

Debasing Ecstasy, Roman Spectacle, and Christ's Ecstatic Forgiveness

The notion of watching torture as a form of entertainment is repulsive to most modern people, which makes it difficult for us to understand how the horrific spectacles that were a feature of daily life in the Roman Empire could ever be understood as an experience of "ecstasy."[27] Nevertheless, ancient Romans did in fact enjoy violent spectacle, including crucifixion. Garrett Fagan remarks, "That the Romans enjoyed watching the games is perhaps so glaringly obvious as to require no documentation";[28] and as we have seen in the works of both Christian and pagan authors, Roman spectators were rapt by the eroticism of the violence, the roar of the crowd, and the indulgence of prejudice against the victims. Seneca, Augustine, Salvian, Livy, Juvenal, Pliny, Tertullian, Martial, and other ancient sources attest to ways Roman spectacles captivated the spectators and held them spellbound.[29]

One particularly striking example of this enjoyment is found in the writings of Seneca, who describes the sheer brutality of the *meridianum spectaculum*, or "midday" spectacle. (Recall here that Caesar Augustus had formalized the scheduling of spectacles in the first century so that animal

27. As we have previously noted, this is the case even though modern people often *enjoy* virtual violence and brutality in movies and video games. Modern people tend to maintain that such enjoyment of violence is different since it is virtual.

28. Fagan, *Lure of the Arena*, 2 n. 4. Fagan further observes that Christian martyriologies are particularly fascinating in the way they convey the enjoyment of the spectators. He notes, for example, how "*The Passion of Perpetua and Felicitas* has been judged a 'public blood bath' that is 'a difficult document to read on many levels'; the same could be said of most of the other martyrologies, and this makes it easy to dismiss spectator behavior as reflecting nothing more than simple barbarity or unvarnished sadism. But they are actually much more interesting texts than that, as they suggest the psychological currents running through the experience of watching execution spectacles in the arena and how people could take enjoyment from it" (*Lure of the Arena*, 256).

29. For a collection of the primary source literature on Roman spectacles, see Mahoney, *Roman Sports and Spectacles*.

hunts [*venatio*] were held in the morning; executions at noon [*meridianum spectaculum*]; and gladiator contests [*munera*] in the afternoon.) Seneca wrote,

> By chance I attended a mid-day exhibition [*meridianum spectaculum*], expecting some fun, wit, and relaxation,—an exhibition at which men's eyes have respite from the slaughter of their fellow-men. But it was quite the reverse. The previous combats were [by comparison] the essence of compassion; but now all the trifling is put aside and it is pure murder. The men have no defensive armor. They are exposed to blows at all points, and no one ever strikes in vain. Many persons prefer this program to the usual pairs and to the bouts "by request" . . . In the morning they throw men to the lions and the bears; at noon, they throw them to the spectators . . . In the morning they cried "Kill him! Lash him! Burn him! . . . Let them receive blow for blow, with chests bare and exposed to the stroke!" And when the games stop for the intermission, they announce: "A little throat-cutting in the meantime, so that there may still be something going on!"[30]

Seneca's description gives us a sense of the Romans' capacity for taking pleasure in seeing other human beings brutally tortured and killed. However, the way in which Romans acted during spectacle entertainments was often different from the way in which they acted in the everyday course of life. As Fagan observes, "Conduct reckoned intolerable when displayed by others in a daily context was condoned in the stands. They would shield their daughters from coarse language, but then expose them to it and use it themselves . . . They would avert their eyes from the corpse of one who had died naturally, but relish the sight of arena victims ripped and lacerated. They would attempt to break up a fight on the street, but applaud far more violent combats in the arena. They would approve of punishment for murder, but then encourage a gladiator to commit murder."[31]

How do we account for such contradictory behavior? Fagan notes that participating in spectacle entertainments corresponded with "an identity shift." Spectators were subjected to the influence of powerful forces. "There can have been few psychological experiences quite like it," writes Fagan, and he points to Augustine's description of Alypius in the Coliseum as an example of the powerful, debasing forces that impinged on individual

---

30. Seneca, *Ep.* 7.3–5, quoted in Kyle, *Spectacles of Death in Ancient Rome*, 91.

31. Fagan, *Lure of the Arena*, 123.

spectators.[32] Though his friends forcefully dragged him into the amphitheater, Alypius was resolved not to participate: "You may drag my body into that place and fix me there, but can you direct my mind and my eyes to the show? I will be there, and yet be absent, and so get the better both of you and of the performance." However, once inside the arena, "a huge roar from the entire crowd beat upon him," and he lost his fortitude. The crowd had a powerful debasing effect on him, cultivating his lower appetites and subjecting him to those appetites. He "gulped in the brutality" and "drank in the frenzy."[33]

Although Augustine does not use the phrase "debasing ecstasy" in his description of Alypius, Aquinas's account of debasing ecstasy describes well what happened to Alypius when he was exposed to the spectacle. Although he was resolved and stalwart against the spectacle, it "pierced" him and "melted" his disposition through the sensuality of his lower appetites. Augustine even describes Alypius as "gulping" and "drinking in" the frenzy of what he saw and heard. He was subsequently "drawn out" of himself and transformed; Augustine says he was "no longer the man who had joined the crowd; he was now one of the crowd he had joined." Fagan suggests that because Augustine's description of Alypius reflects an intimate awareness of the debasing effect of spectacles, Augustine may in fact be describing his own experience (or else projecting his own experience onto Alypius): "The strikingly immediate nature of this account raises justifiable suspicions that Augustine is here describing his own experiences rather than someone else's. He admits elsewhere in his writing that he had once entertained a passion for spectacles, although he is vague about the details."[34] Whether Augustine is describing the inner effect of the spectacle on himself or on his friend Alypius, his description illustrates the potential power of Roman spectacles to subject a person's "intellective appetite" to the urges of his "lower appetite."

Augustine's description of Alypius (or himself, if that be the case) also highlights the way in which the crowd enhanced and contributed to the debasing ecstasy of the spectacle. He says both that Alypius lost his fortitude *because of the crowd* and that he lost himself *to the crowd*. Augustine

32. The experience of Alypius at the Coliseum as described by Augustine plays an important role in Fagan's study of the social psychology of the Roman spectacles. See Fagan, *Lure of the Arena*, 1–10, 122–24, 137, and 292.

33. For Augustine's description of Alypius, see *Confessions*, 146–47.

34. Fagan, *Lure of the Arena*, 1 n. 3.

was not alone in observing that the crowd could carry a person off and out of himself. Like Augustine, Seneca observed the debasing power of crowds at spectacles. Seneca's description of the bloodthirsty spectators at the noonday execution (the *meridianum spectaculum* cited above) is part of an exhortation against the deleterious effects of crowds, and especially of crowds at spectacles. He says,

> To consort with the crowd is harmful; there is no person who does not make some vice attractive to us, or stamp it upon us, or taint us unconsciously therewith. Certainly, the greater the mob with which we mingle, the greater the danger.
>
> But nothing is so damaging to good character as the habit of lounging at the games [spectacles]; for then it is that vice steals subtly upon one through the avenue of pleasure. What do you think I mean? I mean that I come home more greedy, more ambitious, more voluptuous, and even more cruel and inhuman . . . [35]

At spectacle entertainments, the crowd was collectively addressed as *domini* ("lords"). For example, though he was emperor, Claudius addressed the crowd as *dominus*, as did prominent political leaders like Cicero. Fagan writes, "Here, in this time and place, the spectators imagined themselves lords for a day, and were addressed as such. This was their place, where they were the 'masters.'"[36] Regarding the crowds' role as "lords," Fagan further observes how "Seneca's account reveals something of the spectator's mental state. During executions, [the crowd's] ability to direct the course of action on the sand would have strengthened an already formidable sense of empowerment, indeed the ultimate sense of empowerment, over life and death itself. This was one of the clearest manifestations of the crowd as *domini*, lords of the arena."[37] Participating in the lordship of the crowd was a very important aspect of the experience for the spectators, and Fagan points

35. Seneca, *Letters from a Stoic*, 7. See also discussion of this passage in Futrell, *Roman Games*, 118.

36. Fagan, *Lure of the Arena*, 130. An excellent example of the crowd being addressed as *dominus* can be found in the Magerius mosaic, which depicts a hunting spectacle (*venatio*). It shows a herald addressing the crowd, saying, "My Lords, in order that the Telegenii have your favor's reward for each leopard killed, give them five hundred denarii." Fagan observes that while the crowd did not actually give money (this was the responsibility of the sponsor of the spectacle, who was usually a politician or a prominent, wealthy person), nevertheless "the crowd is addressed as if they determine how much the huntsmen are to be paid, as if the crowd had control over the event's sponsor, or as if the two—the crowd and sponsor—were a single unit" (ibid., 130).

37. Ibid., 133.

out that when the victims thwarted this in some way, the crowd would exhibit a "counter-empathic response." For example, when Christian martyrs welcomed the torments of their persecutors, the crowd became enraged because "such behavior challenged the spectators' social identity as 'lords' of the arena . . . this was part of what frustrated and angered them . . . If they [the victims] are smiling or laughing or talking back to the spectators, they do not give much of an impression of suffering, and so the crowd's enjoyment of the proceedings was undermined."[38] In order to enjoy the feeling of being "lords," the crowd needed to experience its power over the victim, and so they would ridicule and hurl insults all the more if the victim did not play along to their liking.

We can see how even a stalwart and intelligent individual like Augustine, Seneca, or Alypius could be carried away by such a crowd. The crowd functioned as a kind of anti-ecclesia, a community of (mal)formation in which debasing ecstasy was mutually reinforced by one's peers. This perverse mutuality encouraged prejudice and scapegoating, especially in the case of executions.[39] As Fagan observes, "Prejudicial attitudes became part and parcel of the crowd's social identity and categorizations, and thus also a part of how the crowd dynamics manifested at that moment . . . Indeed, it was precisely this dynamism and vividness that made the psychological environment [of the spectacles] so powerful."[40]

A quintessential example of prejudice and scapegoating occurs in Tacitus's description of Nero's executions of Christians. The Romans were already prejudiced against this "strange sect" (whom they regarded as atheists), so when a great fire devoured Rome in AD 64, the Christians quickly became scapegoats. Tacitus describes how their executions became great spectacles: "Mockery was added as they died, as they were covered in wild beasts' skins and died torn apart by dogs, or fixed to crosses or, when daylight faded, burned to serve as torches at night. Nero provided his own gardens for the spectacle and put on a show in the circus."[41]

Reading of first-century Christians being mocked and crucified as a spectacle brings to mind the experience of Christ, who was likewise

38. Ibid., 256–57.

39. Fagan says, "To be sure, phases of the spectacle or specific incidents on the sand would have made one or more of the mental processes temporarily more salient than the others—prejudice and counter-empathic emotions coming to the fore during executions, for instance" (*Lure of the Arena*, 284).

40. Ibid.

41. Tacitus *Ann.* 15.44.4–5, cited in Fagan, *Lure of the Arena*, 180.

mocked, crucified, and made a spectacle. The gospel narratives tell us how a multitude was whipped into a frenzy as they shouted, "Crucify him! Crucify him!" Roman soldiers fashioned a thorn of crowns and dressed him in scarlet as they mocked him, saying, "Hail! King of the Jews!" (Matt 27:28–29). From the foot of the cross, soldiers and spectators hurled insults: "Those who passed by derided him, shaking their heads and saying, 'Aha! You who would destroy the temple and build it in three days, save yourself, and come down from the cross!'" (Mark 15:29–30; cf. Matt 27:40, Luke 23:35–36). Christ's crucifixion is a quintessential example of debasing ecstasy. The crowd assumes its role as *domini* in direct opposition to Christ; we see this juxtaposition of lordship explicitly when the Roman soldiers come up to the cross and mock Jesus, saying, "If you are the king of the Jews, save yourself!" (Luke 23:36–37). Even one of the thieves crucified with Jesus assumed the role of spectator and took to mocking him, saying, "Aren't you the Christ? Save yourself and us!" (Luke 23:29; cf. Matt 27:44, Mark 15:32).

In the Gospel of Luke, the mockery of the spectators is juxtaposed with the unconditional forgiveness Christ utters from the cross: "Father, forgive them; for they know not what they do" (Luke 23:34). These words of forgiveness are an example of a "counter-empathic response." Jesus expresses love and concern for the very people who are torturing him, and his prayer challenges the spectators' self-perception as *domini*, as lords overseeing the just punishment of a guilty criminal. Jesus' intercession on their behalf upends this perception by conveying that *they* are the guilty ones in need of forgiveness, and it is *he* who, as their Lord and King, disseminates the forgiveness of the Father. Jesus forgives the spectators as people who "do not know what they do," because they do not understand that he is redeeming them. This forgiveness effects a transformation in the soldiers and the crowd. Luke describes the Roman centurion overseeing Jesus' crucifixion as declaring, "Certainly this man was innocent!" (Luke 23:47); and Luke writes that "the multitudes who came together for this *spectacle*, when they saw what had happened, began to return, beating their breasts" (Luke 23:48 NASB).[42]

42. The Greek word translated "spectacle" in this passage is *theoria*. As per Bauer, et al., it can be translated as "sight" but is used "mostly of public spectacles, religious festivals, processions, etc.," as in "a spectacle for the crowd." For example, it is used in 3 Macc 5:20–24 to describe a violent spectacle: a great crowd gathered to watch with pleasure as the Jews were executed by being trampled by a herd of elephants: "[T]he elephants should be prepared without delay . . . for the extermination of the Jews. When

For historical as well as theological reasons, it is important to note that Jesus's words of forgiveness in Luke 23:34 are not original to Luke, but were most likely added at a later date.[43] Thus, there is little reason to think they represent the actual words of Jesus, but this is no reason to regard them as being of lesser value. Rather, as a redaction, they illuminate Christ's self-giving in terms of redemptive forgiveness. In the Eucharist, Christ offers his body and blood as a gift, and in Luke's narrative, this offering is connected directly with forgiveness and grace. These words of forgiveness are a quintessential example of the forgiver (Christ) embodying what John Milbank describes as the "seeking" of "an ontological harmony" between the forgiver and the forgiven. Such forgiveness is not merely "disinterested benevolence" but involves the forgiver abandoning himself and severing himself from himself for the sake of the forgiven.[44] Milbank observes that such a severing of the self for the sake of the other in the name of forgiveness corresponds to a "relational *ecstasis*," or ecstasy, that is exemplified in the gift of the Eucharist.[45] In the crucifixion, Christ utterly emptied himself of himself for the sake of fallen humanity. He was pierced (literally and figuratively), and he allowed himself to be severed in order that his beloved (humanity) might be joined to him and redeemed. Through the *ecstasis* of this forgiveness, the debasing ecstasy of the spectacle was overaccepted and redirected; the blood of the spectacle became the blood of the New Covenant. The New Covenant signifies an ecstasy, for, as Milbank observes, to forgive out of *ecstasis* is "to restore that order of free unlimited exchange of charity which was interrupted by sin."[46] Thus, *ecstasis* is not a charity that comes to us through an economy of exchange, but through a pure and prevenient grace that exists before we even recognize that it has been offered.[47]

---

the King had spoken, all who were present readily assented together with joy . . . [King] Hermon set the beasts in all their paraphernalia in motion in the great colonnade. The crowds in the city thronged together for the piteous spectacle [*theoria*]." For the text of 3 Macc quoted here, see Charlesworth, *Old Testament Pseudepigrapha*, 2:524. For the use of *theoria* as spectacle, see BADG, 360.

43. New Testament text critics generally agree on the addition of Luke 23:34. For example, Bruce Metzger observes that the absence of these words of Christ from the most reliable and early witnesses "is most impressive" and probably was "incorporated by unknown copyists relatively early in the transmission of the Third Gospel" (Metzger, *Textual Commentary on the Greek New Testament*, 154).

44. Milbank, *Being Reconciled*, 57.

45. Ibid.

46. Ibid.

47. Ibid. Milbank writes, "It might seem . . . that if one forgives in order, or partly

In the Gospel of Luke, we see that an admission of guilt from the spectators is not the necessary condition for their forgiveness; the forgiveness that comes through Christ is not predicated on their contrition but is an effect of Christ's own *ecstasis*—his complete emptying of himself out of his love for them.

Christ's *ecstasis* pertains to what Aquinas describes as a "higher knowledge" that is "outside the connatural apprehension of sense and reason" (cf. *Summa* 1.1 Q 28, Art 3, cited above). It is because of this transcendent knowledge that Jesus says, "they know not what they do." Though the spectators gaze up at him out of their debasement, he gazes down on them in love; and though they consume his body and blood as a spectacle, he offers it as a sacrament. We have already seen how, for Aquinas, the Eucharist pertains to an ecstasy that transforms the believer by piercing his old self and drawing him into love for Christ that transforms him into Christ. This transformation is ongoing; as the believer consumes Christ, he is drawn more and more into the ecstasy of Christ's forgiveness. This transformation by forgiveness makes him a grateful and gracious person who does not desire out of the insatiable void of his soul, for he has been filled with the knowledge that he has received an immeasurable gift of grace that he does not deserve. Thus, he regards other people and creation as a gift rather than as something to be taken for his own pleasure.

The fact that the Christian must regularly consume the Eucharist signifies two important realities. First, the Christian's transformation is always ongoing. Forgiveness does not signify the fullness of reconciliation, and so he is always moving away from insatiable consumption and deeper into the satisfaction of Christ's forgiveness. If he lapses, whether because the spectacle ensnares him or for some other reason, Christ's forgiveness beckons him back with the words, "Take. Eat. Do this in remembrance of me." In *remembering* Christ's gift of grace, the Christian believer is *re-membered* to Christ by taking Christ's body into herself. This consumption heals her soul by piercing and melting the old self with the ecstatic love of and for Christ. Second, in becoming more like Christ, the Christian becomes increasingly able to forgive as Christ forgives. This means that her capacity to forgive

---

in order, to be forgiven, there is a trade in forgiveness such that, after all, Christian forgiveness does not escape the calculative prudence of Greek *aphesia* and Latin *ignoscere*. However, this would be again to overlook the aneconomic economy of pardon. For this economy, to offer charity . . . is not an empty disposition (as it later became), but the ontological bond between God and creatures, whereby creatures only are as the receiving of the divine gift and the unqualified return of this gift in the very act of receiving."

transcends an economy of exchange, and she aspires to a "higher knowledge" that forgives preemptively, without condition, just as Christ does from the cross in Luke. This forgiveness frees her from bitterness and the trappings of past sins and opens her to the transformations of grace and possibility of future reconciliation. Like Christ's forgiveness, this forgiveness does not presume that reconciliation is complete, but it anticipates when (*not if*) it will happen.

It is helpful here to remember how Augustine describes Christ's crucifixion as the "True Spectacle" in order to differentiate between the spectator, who gazes the crucifixion with a debasing ecstasy, and Christ's disciple, who gazes through the ecstasy of forgiveness. For Augustine, the Christian sees the spectacle of Christ's crucifixion with different eyes. He says, "Our interest in one and the same spectacle is quite different from that of the persecutor. He was enjoying the martyr's punishment, we its cause; he was taking pleasure in what he was suffering, we in why he was suffering; he in his torments, we in his strength . . . because he was abiding in the faith."[48] This vision is made possible by the Eucharist, because for Augustine, the Eucharist is the *corpus mysticum Christi* that unifies believers with Christ. Augustine's thinking "admitted no sharp fissure between the real presence of Christ in the bread and the real presence of Christ within the [Christian] community."[49] Thus, gazing on Christ's crucifixion as a spectacle does not debase the Christian's soul but enlightens it and draws him closer to Christ. Moreover, Augustine understands the spectacle as part of God's plan of redemption as foretold in Scripture:

> [Christ] told us himself, before he became a spectacle to be gaped at he foretold it himself, and in prophetic language he declared beforehand what was going to happen as if it already had. He said in the psalm, "They dug my hands and my feet, they counted all my bones" (Ps 22:16–17). There you have how he became a spectacle to be stared at, so that they even counted his bones. He goes on to call it a spectacle even more plainly: "They, however, looked at me closely and stared at me" (Ps 22:17).[50]

Though sinful humanity crucified Christ out of evil desire and debasing ecstasy, God used the spectacle for good and made the cross a sign of God's magnanimous reign.

48. Augustine, *Essential Sermons*, 320.

49. Harmless, *Augustine and the Catechumenate*, 319.

50. Augustine, *Essential Sermons*, 64.

Ultimately, Christ's forgiving *ecstasis* is the sign that even in its most confused and debased state, humanity is not out of reach of God's saving arm. As the psalmist says, "Where can I go from your spirit? Or where can I flee from your presence? If I ascend to heaven you are there; if I make my bed in Sheol, you are there . . . even the darkness is not dark to you; the night is as bright as the day, for darkness is as light to you" (Ps 139:7–8, 12). It is because humanity cannot ultimately separate itself from God that Aquinas says, "Man must, of necessity, desire all, whatsoever he desires, of the last end . . . And if he desire it, not as his perfect good, which is the last end, he must, of necessity, desire it as tending to the perfect good, because the beginning of anything is always ordained to its completion."[51] From the vantage point of Christ's cross, we see that even the debasing ecstasies of Roman spectacles can be seen as reflecting a desire for God.

Having seen how Aquinas's account of ecstasy illuminates the spectacle of Christ's crucifixion, we now turn to the modern spectacle, in which ecstasy continues to play a powerful role in spectacle entertainments. As we look at the social phenomenon of the modern music festival, we will consider how the ecstasy it cultivates in the spectators can also be overaccepted and counted as misdirected longing for God.

From Ancient to Modern Ecstasy: Taking Aquinas to the Music Festival

The Glastonbury Festival of Contemporary Performing Arts is one of the world's great music festivals. Every year, as summer draws to a close, some of the biggest bands in the world take the stage before more than 150,000 spectators. Few bands have taken the main stage more than once, but in 2011 the British band Coldplay headlined the festival for the third time, becoming one of only four bands ever to do so in the festival's forty-year history.[52] As Coldplay began their final song, "Every Teardrop Is a Waterfall," the stage exploded in an enormous laser light show that spread out over the crowd, illuminating the thousands of fans. Like other concerts of this magnitude, Coldplay's performance was a carefully engineered spectacle, a system of signifiers designed to lift the collective soul of the crowd, uniting them in a common experience of rapture. The crowd's thunderous

51. Aquinas, *Summa* 2.1, 1, cited in Williams, 94.

52. The others were Van Morrison, The Cure, and Elvis Costello.

roar filled the night sky as the singer's soaring voice expressed a deep longing to transcend immanence and touch Heaven:

> All the kids they dance
> All the kids all night
> Until Monday morning
> Feels another life
> I turn the music up
> I'm on a roll this time
> *And heaven is in sight*

As the song unfolded, the singer continued to voice an irresistible longing for transcendence. Through the lyrics of the song he boldly claimed that even in his darkness, helplessness, and desperation, humanity can reach for the heavens and discover that cathedrals are in the heart:

> Maybe I'm in the black
> Maybe I'm on my knees
> Maybe I'm in the gap
> Between the two trapezes
> But my heart is beating
> And my pulse is starting
> *Cathedrals in my heart.*

As the song climaxes, the lead singer, who is backed by giant screens that transform his slight frame into a towering and passionate presence dominating the night sky, sings a refrain that declares again and again that *every sign exceeds itself*:

> Every siren is a symphony
> Every teardrop is a waterfall
> It's a waterfall!
> It's a waterfall!
> Every teardrop is a waterfall!

The singer wants to see the world as a collection of signs that point beyond themselves to something greater. He sings of heaven and longs for his immanent existence to be a participation in a transcendent beyond, even if he does not (or cannot) articulate the metaphysical nature of that beyond. The song is like an offering to an "Unknown God," and it resonated strongly with the thousands of spectators at the concert. Moreover, it resonates with millions of Coldplay fans around the globe.

There is nothing exceptional about the Glastonbury Festival or the performance of Coldplay that is not readily observable at similar music

festivals and concerts throughout the world. Other examples include Lalla-
palooza in Chicago, Illinois (which attracts more than 160,000 people over
a period of three days) and Bumpershoot in Seattle, Washington (which
gathers more than 100,000 at the Seattle Center). More examples can be
found in Australia, Japan, South Africa, Brazil, and Europe. Such festivals
are carefully constructed symbolic systems designed to enable the spectator
to have experiences of ecstasy so wonderful and powerful that they are difficult to capture with words. Euphoria washes in waves over the enormous
crowds, and with raised hands the spectators wave, yell, and scream lyrics
that most of them know by heart. This ecstasy is facilitated by a great sense
of belonging and mutuality that comes from participating as a member of
the enormous crowd of spectators. This belonging coincides with a complete absence of personal space. Bodies are crammed so closely together
that everyone is touching someone else, and an overt sexual tension perme-
ates the air.

This ecstasy comes at great financial expense. The bands, stages, special effects, crowd control, ticketing, and marketing are all paid for by corporate sponsors, which—knowing the market value of having their brands
associated with such euphoric experience—gladly fork over millions of
dollars. These corporate brands are displayed above the stages and in other
prominent places where consumers can see them. Many festivals and concerts, like the V Festival in England, are named for their sponsors. (The
V in V Festival stands for the Virgin venture capital conglomerate, which
includes Virgin Mobile and Virgin Music among its many subsidiaries.) It
is not only the sponsors that have brands; the performers themselves have
been carefully branded according to certain molds and marketing strategies
designed to make spectacles of them. Stars are constantly being produced
so that when the flame of an iconic pop star eventually burns out, she can
quickly be replaced by a new starlet—and the cycle begins anew. However,
continuing the cycle does not happen automatically. Enormous amounts of
money must be invested in creating a new spectacle for the new performer.
By following proven methods, corporations can protect their investment,
and as Jan Jagodzinski observes, this investment ultimately pays off as
"power becomes concentrated in the record companies, and producers who
front the spectacle and invest time and money in it."[53]

Spectacles designed to promote performers in the media work sym-
biotically with the spectacle of the live concert. The media spectacle makes

53. Jagodzinski, *Music in Youth Culture*, 3.

the performers seem transcendent to their adoring fans. Ordinarily fans have access to the performer only through the spectacles of the media, but at concerts the fans experience a physical proximity with the performer's transcendence. A great deal of engineering and effort goes into maintaining the transcendence of the performers while they are on stage. They are surrounded by laser light shows and their image is projected on enormous screens, making them appear larger than life and superhuman. Many performers like to play with this perception of transcendence by selecting a fan from the crowd and bringing him onto the stage. The visual juxtaposition of the performer (who is more than comfortable on stage) with the fan (who is stunned to find himself face to face with the performer and on a stage before tens of thousands of his peers) heightens the image of the performer as a transcendent figure. For example, during the performance of one of U2's most iconic songs, Bono, the lead singer, selected a female fan and lay down with her on the stage. After cuddling her for several minutes, and finally kissing her on the mouth, he returned her to the audience. This event was professionally recorded for one of U2's DVDs and is admired by fans of U2 around the world. It has been viewed more than thirty million times on YouTube.[54] The experience clearly induced a powerful ecstasy in the fan and left many of the other spectators longing to have the same experience with their idol.

What is particularly interesting about this example of ecstasy is that it is the byproduct of a quasi-incarnational metaphysics. The overwhelming majority of Bono's fans know him primarily through the transcendence of the spectacle created by the media (i.e., MTV and similar venues), but at the concert he is present among his fans in the flesh. So when Bono lies down with one of the fans, holding and kissing her, it is as if he has descended from on high to be close to the fans as one who deeply cares for them. To do this with one fan is to do it symbolically with all of them. Even if a fan cannot be the lucky one caressed by Bono, the fan nevertheless feels and senses the significance of this physical encounter as a connection with the transcendence Bono represents. A transcendent performer who is with fans in the flesh provides them with a sense of Immanuel: a god is with us.[55] This quasi-incarnational metaphysics is a quintessential example

54. See http://www.youtube.com/watch?v=_Ye8GLPUVsM.

55. It should be noted here that there is nothing extraordinary about Bono's interaction with his fans that is not readily observable in other performers. Most pop stars follow the same patterns.

of how the society of the spectacle has not vanquished the theological but rather imitates it as simulacra. Moreover, it illustrates how the innate human longing for Incarnation has not disappeared from Western society, but has actually found a new outlet in the spectacles of consumer culture.

This observation is of strategic significance for the many churches trying to reach today's so-called secular young people. Young people may be absent from the church's pews, but this is *not* because young people have been secularized. Rather, they exhibit a deep and profound longing for transcendence, ecstatic experience, mutuality, and even incarnational metaphysics. When they cannot experience their favorite performers in the flesh, they can make do with recorded music. iPods and MP3 players provide them with immediate access to ecstatic experience; the young person can put on his headphones, tune out the world, and let himself be carried away. As Kenda Creasy Dean observes, youth "crave transcendence . . . not because they have no other gods to choose from but because they have *so many* to choose from . . . If God is 'whatever moves me,' then any transporting experience—from orgasm to thrill seeking to dropping acid —feels 'spiritual,' at least temporarily."[56] Spectacle reaches deep into the souls of young people and connects with youthful passion and potential. It cultivates their desires with promises of transporting experiences and articulates their search for identity and meaning in terms of consumption.

In his article "The Beauty of the Metaphysical Imagination," John Betz articulates the relationship between metaphysics and aesthetics in ways that help further illuminate the metaphysics of the music festival.[57] Following Aquinas and John Milbank, Betz observes how "[B]eautiful things—more so than ordinary things—display an excess of their appearing. In short, they daze us with their depth" and open our eyes to the ways in which visible reality "becomes a site of the appearing of the invisible."[58] The spectacle of the concert immerses the spectator in a certain kind of beauty that dazzles her, opens her eyes, and makes her aware of this metaphysical depth. Though she cannot articulate this, she senses it, for it has cultivated a longing for transcendence and ecstasy within her. Betz observes that Aquinas's doctrine of the *analogia entis* is essentially a way of accounting for this experience of metaphysical depth: "what the *analogia entis* seeks to describe . . .

56. Dean, *Practicing Passion*, 101, 113. My italics.

57. Betz, "Beauty of the Metaphysical Imagination."

58. Ibid., 61.

is altogether akin to what we feel in the face of beauty."[59] It is a "metaphysical expression for aesthetic experience: of the fact that there is an alluring depth to things that is never reducible to the things themselves."[60] From this perspective it becomes possible to see how the aesthetics of the concert allow spectators to *experience a simulacra of the analogia entis* even if they are not able to articulate that this is what is happening. Through the concert, they become aware of themselves as finite beings whose existence reflects a desire for an unnamed transcendence. Although the quasi-incarnational metaphysics of the performer who descends to be an Immanuel for his fans is a mere simulacra of the true Incarnation, it nevertheless signifies a deep longing for the true Incarnation. The same can be said of the sexual objectification, violence, drug use, and other destructive desires that concerts and music festivals often cultivate in the spectators. As we have seen, even when a spectacle produces a debasing ecstasy in the spectators (as it did in Rome's spectacles entertainments and at Golgotha), this ecstasy can be understood as a misguided desire for God. Even when a young spectator tries to enhance her experience of the music festival by becoming wildly drunk, we should remember that Aquinas speaks of the eucharistic ecstasy as inebriation. Whatever the form of misdirected desire, Aquinas reminds us that "man must, of necessity, desire all, whatsoever he desires, of the last end . . . And if he desire it, not as his perfect good, which is the last end, he must, of necessity, desire it as tending to the perfect good, because the beginning of anything is always ordained to its completion."[61]

Transgressing the Secular

The foregoing analysis transgresses the secular by using a theological metaphysics to articulate contemporary music concerts as experiences of the *analogia entis* and a quasi-incarnational metaphysics. As we close this chapter, I want to offer this transgression as a paradigmatic strategy for the church's engagement with the society of the spectacle. The epistemologies of modernity and the antimetaphysical, immanent ontologies of postmodernity (Heidegger et al.) attempt to secure a secular space that limits and quarantines the theological by categorizing Christianity as "religion." As the influence and pressures of secularizing modernity have grown over the

59. Ibid., 62.

60. Ibid.

61. Aquinas, *Summa* 2.1, 1, cited in Williams, *Ground of Union*, 94.

last century, Christianity has learned, for various reasons and in various ways, to accept this quarantining. So long as Christianity resigns itself to its proper place in modern Western society—so long as it stays locked in the cage fashioned for it by secularism and consumer culture—it cannot articulate the gospel as the salvation of all humanity. Thus, it has been the purpose of this chapter not only to release Christianity from the cage of secularism but to show, by employing a theological metaphysics, that the cage is an illusion. This becomes clear once we begin to see that so-called secular Western culture has really not culminated in postmetaphysical social life but in a modern society of the spectacle that exhibits a deep longing for transcendence and that mediates social life metaphysically.

In *Theology and Social Theory,* John Milbank says, "Once there was no secular."[62] To this statement we add a brief addendum: secularism really never has been, because human beings, even in their most debased state, express a desire and longing for God. This is not to say that there has not been something called secularism, but that at the end of the day secularism really isn't possible. Its possibility is an illusion because human beings are made in the image of God, and a person "must, of necessity, desire all, whatsoever he desires, of the last end." And even when our desires are debased—even if we cry, "Crucify him! Crucify Him!"—they reflect a misguided longing for God. Because the efficacy of Christ's forgiveness is grounded in his *ecstasis* (his utter abandonment of himself for our sake) and is not contingent on our contrition, there is no one who is out of his reach. This is for God's glory, a sign of God's absolute sovereignty, and it is also for our benefit.

Our analysis of the music festival serves as an example of this point, but more importantly, it represents the kind of articulation in which the church and contemporary theology should engage in order to strip away the illusion of secularism. Theological metaphysics is not merely theoretical but also very practical and should be a foremost discipline for the training of clergy. A pastor or theologian who can help a Consumer Subject recognize his misdirected longing for God in his insatiable desire and acts of consumption is a pastor who can engage the society of the spectacle.

As the central act of Christian worship, the Eucharist provides Christian believers with an alternative understanding of consumption whereby we (re)discover ourselves as creatures whose lives are made possible by the supreme gifts of Christ's grace. This grace shapes our vision of the world

62. Milbank, *Theology and Social Theory,* 9.

and our interactions with it. However, it is also important to remember what we have learned from Augustine and early Christianity: that the Eucharist requires preparation and exorcism. Because we live in the society of the spectacle, our desires are distorted by the demonic, and in the course of this volume we have sought to articulate what this means for today. Augustine's understanding of the demonic continues to be pertinent as Christians wrestle with the principalities of the modern society of the spectacle. However, this does not mean that we can simply transplant the early church's practices of ritual exorcism into our context; rather, we have to creatively and carefully cultivate practices of dehabituation that attend to the particular manifestations of the demonic in the modern society of the spectacle. The ecstasy of forgiveness should play an important role in this dehabituation, for contemplating the supreme gift of Christ's forgiveness can pierce and melt the old self so that we can be drawn into newness. Then we will be ready and able to receive Christ's gift of himself and be transformed into his likeness, into the body of Christ.

5

Conclusion

CONTESTING FOR CHRISTIANITY

A great theater is filled with spectators to watch your contests and your
summons to martyrdom, just as if we were to speak of a great crowd
gathered to watch the contests of athletes supposed to be champions. . .
the whole world and all the angels of the right and left, and all men,
those from God's portion and those from the other portions, will attend
to us when we contest for Christianity.

—ORIGEN[1]

In 2004 journalist Douglass Rushkoff produced a *Frontline* documentary
for PBS called *The Persuaders*, which investigated the methodologies and
practices of modern marketing.[2] In the course of their research, Rushkoff
and his team interviewed marketers from some of the world's largest advertising firms, and what they found surprised them: leading brand manag-
ers were trying to create cult brands (like Apple, Nike, Starbucks, etc.) by
studying religious cults. Douglas Atkin, of Merkely + Partners Advertising,
told Rushkoff,

---

1. Origen, *Exhortation to Martyrdom*, quoted in Young, *In Procession Before the
World*, 54.

2. Douglass Rushkoff is an author, scholar, and documentarian, and a correspondent
and producer for *Frontline*. For more of his work, see www.rushkoff.com.

The "aha moment" came when I was looking at eight individuals rhapsodizing about a sneaker in a research facility in New York one cold night, and these people were using the kind of evangelical terms and vocabulary you might expect from a cult meeting or a revivalist meeting. I mean, these people were converts. I was thinking, where is this coming from? Why are these people so committed? This is incredibly ironic, because I had just come from a meeting of colleagues and marketers where everyone had been wringing their hands about how brand loyalty was dead. Well, clearly it wasn't for these people. These people had become unreasonably attracted and attached to what at the end of the day was a piece of footwear.[3]

In light of these questions, Atkin conducted marketing research by doing focus groups with members of Falun Gong, Hare Krishna, and dozens of other cult organizations. He wanted to understand what "pushed a person from mere fan to devoted disciple." Atkins described his finding to Rushkoff, saying, "The conclusion is this: people, whether they are joining a religious cult or a brand, do so for exactly the same reasons. They need to belong, and they want to make meaning. They need to know what the world is all about and they need the company of others." Atkin emphasized that filling this need is at the heart of advertising, and he likened the vocation of brand manager to that of a religious leader, saying, "Now a brand manager has an entirely different kind of responsibility. In fact, they have more responsibility. Their job now is to create and maintain a whole meaning system for people through which they get [their] identity and understanding of the world. Their job now is to be a community leader." Rushkoff's conversations with marketers like Atkin caused him to realize that marketers have crossed the boundary separating the sacred and the secular. He observed that today advertisers "fill the empty spaces where . . . churches once did the job."

The Persuaders illustrates one of the key insights of our study, which is that the society of the spectacle is the expression of religious longing. Guy Debord observed that modern consumption has taken on a transcendent quality and that "consumers are filled with religious fervor."[4] A person trying to free himself from the society of the spectacle is very much like a religious person trying to stop believing in God. One would expect this

3. For the transcript of Rushkoff's interview with Atkin, see http://www.pbs.org/wgbh/pages/frontline/shows/persuaders/interviews/atkin.html.

4. Debord, *Society of the Spectacle*, 14.

observation to lead Debord to assess the theological and metaphysical nuances of the society of the spectacle, but as a neo-Marxist, his view of religion was simplistic and resolutely negative. He regarded religion as the "opiate of the masses" and argued that spectacle, like religion, undercuts political subjectivity by "keep[ing] people in a state of unconsciousness as they pass through practical changes in their conditions."[5] The society of the spectacle, he said, is merely the "reconstruction of the religious illusion"[6]

In contrast to Debord, this study has sought to assess the theological and metaphysical nuances of the society of the spectacle and their impact on social and political life. We have done this by recovering the practices and theological metaphysics of early Christians who lived in the shadow of Rome's spectacle entertainments. Early Christians such as Augustine recognized that Roman spectacles were fully integrated with Rome's cultic system and that "all spectacle began as elaborate celebrations of the divine powers."[7] By means of the *pompa*, the Romans paraded the images of their gods and deified emperors into the amphitheater to signify divine presence and approval of the spectacles. Although he regarded these gods as mere idols of human making, Augustine recognized that pagan worship nevertheless had a powerful effect on Rome's social and political life. He articulated this power in metaphysical terms and as the influence of the demonic. In *City of God*, he showed how the worship of the demonic cultivated a love of spectacle, and he described demons as composite beings existing between immanence and transcendence. Augustine said that like God, demons are immortal and exist in the spiritual realm, but like humanity they possess bodies and are fallen beings. Because they are fallen beings, they exhibit the passions of the soul, but because their bodies are perfect and incorruptible, they indulge their lusts without consequence or limit.

In the course of our study, we have seen how Augustine's notion of the demonic sheds light on the metaphysical dimensions of today's consumer culture. Like Rome's society of the spectacle, the modern society of the spectacle is deeply invested in demonic metaphysics. It portrays heaven as a place of insatiable desire where perfect and immortal bodies indulge in the passions of the soul without consequence or limit. With the help of cultural theorists like W. J. T. Mitchell, we have seen how images play an important role in this metaphysics. The images of modern advertising, for example,

---

5. Ibid.

6. Ibid.

7. Futrell, *Roman Games*, 87.

function iconographically. The consumer participates analogically in the metaphysical ideals the image represents, for the image functions as a *modus significandi*, and the act of consuming is his *modus operandi*. As an accumulated whole, the images of the society of the spectacle constitute a massive symbolic order with which the consumer interacts to make meaning. As brand manager Douglas Atkin keenly discerned in his focus group studies, consumers "need to belong, and they want to make meaning. They need to know what the world is all about and they need the company of others." However, consumers are saturated with diverse and competing messages, all vying for their devotion and allegiance. The society of the spectacle loves diversity and pluralism, and the consumer is a polytheist who chooses from the many gods available to him according to his personal preferences. Just as there were many deities in the Roman pantheon, there are many gods in the marketplace that represent the particular personalities and values of the consumer. However, as Augustine rightly perceived, this diversity of divinity is an illusion, for all these gods are really just demons that form consumers into their own demonic image by making them subjects of insatiable desire.

For Augustine, a demon is an angelic being engaged in rebellion against God. Thus, for a demon, freedom means the capacity to do whatever one wants, in whatever *way* one wants, and for whatever *reasons* one wants. This notion of freedom is pervasive in the society of the spectacle, and one of the aims of our analysis has been to show its effects on political subjectivity and electoral politics. Democracy was birthed from the Kantian conviction that a democratic citizen was free because he was ruled by Reason (as a transcendental) rather than by a monarch. His democratic freedoms were contingent on obedience to Reason. Today's democratic citizen, on the other hand, does not regard his freedoms as contingent on obedience to Reason. This has had a great impact on the actual functioning of liberal democracy, because the demos is no longer comprised of Citizen Subjects, who exhibit a profound sense of duty and honor, but of Consumer Subjects, who regard their elected officials as service providers and entertainers. Consequently, politicians are compelled by the *vox ominum*, the roar of the crowd, and contemporary politics reflects the sociology of the Roman arena. The electoral process has become a parody of itself—just another reality television show in which the contestant-politicians vie for the affections and votes of the consumer-spectators.

The loss of transcendental metaphysics and subsequent degradation of modern democracy has motivated neo-Marxist scholars like Hardt, Negri, and Surin to articulate the ontological foundations for a new political subjectivity. Hardt and Negri seek an ontological basis of antagonism and a material religion whereby

> the powers of creation that had previously been consigned exclusively to the heavens are now brought down to earth. This is the discovery of the fullness of the plane of immanence . . . Our pilgrimage on earth . . . in contrast to Augustine's has no transcendent *telos* beyond; it is and remains absolutely immanent . . . there is no God the Father and no transcendence. Instead there is our immanent labor . . . .The multitude has no reason to look outside its own history and its own present productive power . . . .To the metaphysical and transcendent mediations are thus opposed the absolute constitution of labor and cooperation, the earthly city of the multitude.[8]

Hardt and Negri insist on an immanent ontology because they hold that all appeals to transcendence are illusory and incapable of producing the kind of political subjectivity necessary for resisting the new mode of Empire. However, there is no reason to accept this assertion, especially when Hardt and Negri readily admit that early Christianity did in fact produce "a new ontological basis" that exhibited "an enormous potential of subjectivity" and "challenged [the Roman Empire] in its totality by a completely different ethical and ontological axis."[9] Early Christians did not achieve this *despite* their theological metaphysics, but *because of* their theological metaphysics. A theological metaphysics that understands human beings as recipients of Christ's grace and agents of the triune God is not merely religious fervor but the ontological foundation for a political subjectivity grounded in *truth*. In the days of the Roman Empire, this ontological foundation was a powerful force against the idolatries and demonic metaphysics of the society of the spectacle, and it can be equally powerful today.

The problem with Hardt and Negri's "material religion" is that it amounts to spiritual austerity that starves the soul of its innate need for God.[10] In this sense, it is merely the flip side of the society of the spectacle: whereas the spectacle malnourishes the soul with demonic metaphysics, the spiritual austerity of neo-Marxism starves the soul by denying it ac-

8. Hardt and Negri, *Empire*, 73–74, 396.

9. Ibid., 396.

10. Ibid.

cess to any transcendence whatsoever. Hardt and Negri do not realize that humanity can no more deny its need for spiritual nourishment than it can deny its need for physical sustenance. Thus, the question that has been at the center of our study is not whether the soul needs transcendence, but how we, as beings made in the image of God, seek after spiritual nourishment. As we have seen, the society of the spectacle is the spiritual equivalent of fast food; its empty calories ultimately leave the consumer longing for the sustenance of the Eucharist.

This brings us to one final point. The society of the spectacle constantly entices with debasing ecstasies—glittering and poisoned gifts that lead us far from God. Yet even when our desires are corrupt and degraded, they nevertheless reflect our true longing, for as Aquinas says, "Man must, of necessity desire all, whatsoever he desires, of the last end . . . And if he desire it, not as his perfect good, which is the last end, he must, of necessity, desire it as tending to the perfect good, because the beginning of anything is always ordained to its completion."[11] By becoming a spectacle, Christ took humanity's sinfulness upon himself and turned our most debased desires toward their preordained end. Christ accomplished this through the sacramental metaphysics of the Eucharist. The person who sees Christ's crucifixion through the sacramental metaphysics of the Eucharist has his desires mediated by a new and different reality. For him, Christ's broken body and spilled blood are not the byproducts of violent spectacle but signs of grace, forgiveness, and salvation. This is why Augustine says of the crucifixion, "Our interest in one and the same spectacle is quite different from that of the persecutor."[12] Thus, for the Christian, Christ is the True Spectacle, and the cross is the sign of God's magnanimous reign.

11. Aquinas, *Summa* I-II, 1, cited in Williams, *Ground of Union*, 94.

12. Augustine, *Essential Sermons*, 320.

Bibliography

Annenberg Public Policy Center. "Partisan Judicial Elections Foster Cynicism and Distrust." http://www.annenbergpublicpolicycenter.org/partisan-judicial-elections-foster-cynicism-and-distrust/.

Ambrose, Saint. *On Mysteries*, New Advent. www.newadvent.org/fathers/3405. htmnewadvent.org.

Augustine, Saint. *City of God*. Translated by Henry Bettenson. New York: Penguin, 1972.

———. *The Confessions*. Translated by Maria Boulding. New York: New City, 1997.

———. *Essential Sermons*. Edited by Boniface Ramsey. Translated by Edmund Hill. New York: New City, 2007.

Badiou, Alain. "The Democratic Emblem." In Giorgio Agamben et al., *Democracy in What State?*, 6–15. New York: Columbia University Press, 2011.

Baudrillard, Jean. *The Intelligence of Evil or the Lucidity Pact*. Translated by Chris Turner. New York: Berg, 2005.

———. *The Perfect Crime*. Translated by Chris Turner. London: Verso, 2008.

Barton, Carlin. A. "Savage Miracle: Redemption of Lost Honor in Roman Society and the Sacrament of the Gladiator and the Martyr." *Representations* 45 (1994) 41–71.

Beacham, Richard. *Spectacle Entertainments of Early Imperial Rome*. New Haven: Yale University Press, 1999.

Benson, Bruce Ellis, and Peter Goodwin Heltzel, eds. *Evangelicals and Empire: Christian Alternatives to the Political Status Quo*. Grand Rapids: Brazos, 2008.

Betz, John R. "The Beauty of the Metaphysical Imagination." In *Belief and Metaphysics*, edited by Conor Cunningham and Peter M Candler, 41–65. London: SCM, 2007.

Bomgardner, David Lee. *The Story of the Roman Amphitheatre*. London: Routledge, 2000.

Brown, Wendy. "We Are All Democrats Now . . ." In Giorgio Agamben et al., *Democracy in What State?*, 44–57. New York: Columbia University Press, 2011.

Cavanaugh, William T. *Being Consumed: Economics and Christian Desire*. Grand Rapids: Erdmans, 2008.

———. *Torture and Eucharist*. Oxford: Blackwell, 1998.

Charlesworth, James H. *The Old Testament Pseudepigrapha and the New Testament: Prolegomena for the Study of Christian Origins*. Cambridge: Cambridge University Press, 1985.

Chase, Kenneth R., and Alan Jacobs, eds. *Must Christianity Be Violent? Reflections on History, Practice, and Theology*. Grand Rapids: Brazos, 2003.

Claiborne, Shane. *The Irresistible Revolution: Living as an Ordinary Radical*. Grand Rapids: Zondervan, 2006.

Crary, Jonathan. *Suspensions of Perception: Attention, Spectacle, and Modern Culture.* Cambridge: MIT Press, 1999.

Dean, Kenda Creasy. *Practicing Passion: Youth and the Quest for a Passionate Church.* Grand Rapids: Eerdmans, 2004.

Debord, Guy. *Society of the Spectacle.* Translated by Ken Knabb. London: AK, 2006.

Desmond, William. *Being and the Between.* Albany: State University of New York Press, 1995.

———. *Ethics and the Between.* Albany: State University of New York Press, 2000.

———. *God and the Between.* Malden, MA: Blackwell, 2008.

———. "Neither Sovereignty nor Servility: Between Politics and Metaphysics." In *Theology and the Political: The New Debate,* edited by Creston Davis, John Milbank, and Slavoj Žižek, 153–82. Durham: Duke University Press, 2005.

Dostoyevsky, Fyodor. *The Brothers Karamazov.* Translated by Richard Pevear and Larissa Volokhonsky. New York: First Vintage Classics, 1991.

Fagan, Garrett G. *The Lure of the Arena: Social Psychology and the Crowd at the Roman Games.* New York: Cambridge University Press, 2011.

Finn, Thomas Macy. "It Happened One Saturday Night: Ritual and Conversion in Augustine's North Africa." *Journal of the American Academy of Religion* 58 (1990) 589–616.

Futrell, Alison, ed. *Blood in the Arena: The Spectacle of Roman Power.* Austin: University of Texas, 1997.

———. *The Roman Games: Historical Sources in Translation* Oxford: Blackwell, 2006.

Galvao, Vinicius. "Clearing the Air." Transcript of interview with Bob Garfield. *On the Media,* April 20, 2007. http://onthemedia.org/transcripts/2007/04/20/04.

Gardner, Lloyd, and Marilyn Young, eds. *The New American Empire: A 21st Century Teach-In on U.S. Foreign Policy.* New York: New Press, 2005.

Girard, René. *I See Satan Fall Like Lightning.* Translated by James G. Williams. Maryknoll, NY: Orbis, 2006.

Guyer, Paul, ed. *The Cambridge Companion to Kant.* Cambridge: Cambridge University Press, 1992.

Hardt, Michael, and Antonio Negri. *Empire.* Cambridge: Harvard University Press, 2001.

———. *Multitude: War and Democracy in the Age of Empire.* New York: Penguin, 2004.

Harmless, William. *Augustine and the Catechumenate.* Collegeville, MN: Pueblo, 1995.

Hart, David Bentley. *The Beauty of the Infinite: The Aesthetics of Christian Truth.* Grand Rapids: Eerdmans, 2004.

Hauerwas, Stanley. *The Hauerwas Reader.* Edited by John Berkman and Michael Cartwright. Durham: Duke University Press, 2001.

Heilemann, John, and Mark Halperin. *Game Change: Obama and the Clintons, McCain and Palin, and the Race of a Lifetime.* New York: Harper, 2010.

Ignatius of Antioch. *Epistle to the Romans,* New Advent. http://www.newadvent.org/fathers/0107.htm.

Jagodzinski, Jan. *Music in Youth Culture: A Lacanian Approach.* New York: Palgrave Macmillian, 2006.

Jowett, Garth S., and Victoria O'Donnell. *Propaganda and Persuasion.* Thousand Oaks, CA: Sage, 2006.

Kant, Immanuel. "Idea for a Universal History with a Cosmopolitan Purpose." In *Kant: Political Writings,* edited by H. S. Reiss, 41–53. Cambridge: Cambridge University Press, 1991.

Kretzmann, Norman. "Philosophy of Mind." In *The Cambridge Companion to Aquinas*, edited by Eleonore Stump and Norman Kretzmann, 128–59. Cambridge: Cambridge University Press, 1993.

Kwasniewski, Peter. "The Ecstasy of Love in Aquinas's *Commentary on the Sentences*." *Angelicum* 83 (2006) 51–93.

———. "St. Thomas on Eucharistic Ecstasy." In *The Liturgical Subject: Subject, Subjectivity, and the Human Person in Contemporary Liturgical Discussion and Critique*, edited by James G. Leachman, 154–71. Notre Dame: University of Notre Dame Press, 2009.

Kyle, Donald G. *Spectacles of Death in Ancient Rome*. New York: Routledge, 1998.

———. *Sport and Spectacle in the Ancient World*. Oxford: Blackwell, 2007.

Lane Fox, Robin. *Pagans and Christians*. New York: Knopf, 1986.

Leachman, James G., ed. *The Liturgical Subject: Subject, Subjectivity, and the Human Person in Contemporary Liturgical Discussion and Critique*. Notre Dame: University of Notre Dame Press, 2009.

Levering, Matthew. *Scripture and Metaphysics: Aquinas and the Renewal of Trinitarian Theology*. Oxford: Blackwell, 2004.

Long, Stephen D. *The Goodness of God: Theology, the Church, and the Social Order*. Grand Rapids: Brazos, 2001.

———. "Radical Orthodoxy." In *The Cambridge Companion to Postmodern Theology*, edited by Kevin J. Vanhoozer, 126–45. Cambridge: Cambridge University Press, 2003.

———. *Speaking of God: Theology, Language, and Truth*. Grand Rapids: Eerdmans, 2009.

Mahoney, Anne. *Roman Sports and Spectacles: A Sourcebook*. Newburyport, MA: Focus, 2001.

Metzger, Bruce M. *A Textual Commentary on the Greek New Testament*. New York: United Bible Societies, 1994.

Milbank, John. *Being Reconciled: Ontology and Pardon*. London: Routledge, 2003.

———. *Theology and Social Theory*. 2nd ed. Oxford: Blackwell, 2006.

Milbank, John, Graham Ward, and Catherine Pickstock. "Introduction: Suspending the Material: The Turn of Radical Orthodoxy." In *Radical Orthodoxy: A New Theology*, edited by John Milbank, Catherine Pickstock, and Graham Ward, 1–19. London: Routledge, 1999.

Mitchell, W. J. T. *What Do Pictures Want? The Lives and Loves of Images*. Chicago: University of Chicago Press, 2005.

Negri, Antonio. "The Political Subject and Absolute Immanence." In *Theology and the Political: The New Debate*, edited by Creston Davis, John Milbank, and Slavoj Žižek, 231–39. Durham: Duke University Press, 2005.

O'Donovan, Oliver, and Joan Lockwood O'Donovan, eds. *From Irenaeus to Grotius: A Sourcebook in Christian Political Thought, 100–1625*. Grand Rapids: Eerdmans, 1999.

Passavant, Paul, and Jodi Dean, eds. *Empire's New Clothes: Reading Hardt and Negri*. New York: Routledge, 2004.

Pickstock, Catherine. *After Writing: The Liturgical Consummation of Philosophy* Oxford: Blackwell, 1998.

———. "The Univocalist Mode of Production." In *Theology and the Political: The New Debate*, edited by Creston Davis, John Milbank, and Slavoj Žižek, 281–325. Durham: Duke University Press, 2005.

Plass, Paul. *The Game of Death in Ancient Rome: Arena Sport and Political Suicide*. Madison: University of Wisconsin Press, 1995.

Quodvultdeus, Bishop of Carthage. *Quodvultdeus of Carthage: The Creedal Homilies.* Translated by Thomas Macy Finn. New York: Newman Press, 2004.

Ranciere, Jacques. *The Emancipated Spectator.* New York: Verso, 2009.

Richmond, Shane. "Call of Duty: Modern Warfare 3 Breaks Sales Records." *The Telegraph*, November 11, 2011. http://www.telegraph.co.uk/technology/video-games/video-game-news/8884726/Call-of-Duty-Modern-Warfare-3-breaks-sales-records.html.

Sager, Ira, and Peter Burrows, with Andy Reinhardt. "Back to the Future at Apple." *Businessweek*, May 25, 1998. http://www.businessweek.com/stories/1998-05-24/back-to-the-future-at-apple.

Saul, John Ralston. *Voltaire's Bastards: The Dictatorship of Reason in the West.* New York: Random House, 1992.

Shaper, Eva. "Taste, Sublimity, and Genius: The Aesthetics of Nature and Art." In *The Cambridge Companion to Kant*, edited by Paul Guyer, 367–94. Cambridge: Cambridge University Press, 1992.

Sloterdijk, Peter, with Hans-Jürgen Heinrichs. *Neither Sun Nor Death.* Translated by Steve Corcoran. Los Angeles: Semiotext(e), 2011.

Smith, Christian, with Patricia Snell. *Souls in Transition: The Religious and Spiritual Lives of Emerging Adults.* Oxford: Oxford University Press, 2009.

Smith, James K. A. *Desiring the Kingdom: Worship, Worldview and Cultural Formation.* Grand Rapids: Baker Academic, 2009.

———. "The Gospel of Freedom, or Another Gospel? Augustinian Reflections on Empire and American Foreign Policy." *Political Theology* 10 (2009) 513–36.

Surin, Ken. *Freedom Not Yet: Liberation and the Next World Order.* Durham: Duke University Press, 2009.

———. "Rewriting the Ontological Script of Liberation: On the Question of Finding a New Political Subject." In *Theology and the Political: The New Debate*, edited by Creston Davis, John Milbank, and Slavoj Žižek, 240–66. Durham: Duke University Press, 2005.

Tertullian. *On Baptism.* In vol. 3 of *Ante-Nicene Fathers.* Translated by S. Thelwal. Grand Rapids: Eerdmans, 1997.

———. *On Spectacles.* In vol. 3 of *Ante-Nicene Fathers.* Translated by S. Thelwal. Grand Rapids: Eerdmans, 1997.

Thomas, Aquinas, Saint. *Basic Writings of St. Thomas Aquinas.* Edited by Anton C. Pegis. Vol. 1. Indianapolis: Hackett, 1997.

Tiqqun. *Preliminary Materials for a Theory of the Young-Girl.* Translated by Ariana Reines. Los Angeles: Semiotext(e), 2012.

Tuplin, Andrew. "Virtual Morality." *Adbusters*, November/December 2008, 82.

Veyne, Paul. *Bread and Circuses: Historical Sociology and Political Pluralism.* Translated by Brian Pearce. New York: Penguin, 1995.

Vanhoozer, Kevin J., ed. *The Cambridge Companion to Postmodern Theology.* Cambridge: Cambridge University Press, 2003.

Ward, Graham. *Cities of God.* London: Routledge, 2000.

Wells, Samuel. *Improvisation: The Drama of Christian Ethics.* Grand Rapids: Brazos, 2004.

Whiston, William, trans. *The Works of Josephus: Complete and Unabridged.* Peabody, MA: Hendrickson, 1995.

Williams, A. N. *The Ground of Union: Deification in Aquinas and Palamas.* New York: Oxford University Press, 1999.

Wroe, Ann. *Pontius Pilate.* New York: Random House, 2001.

Yakobson, A. "*Petitio et Largitio*: Popular Participation in the Centuriate Assembly of the Late Republic." *Journal of Roman Studies* 82 (1992) 32–52.

Yonge, C. D., trans. *The Works of Philo: Complete and Unabridged*. Peabody, MA: Hendrickson, 1993.

Young, Robin Darling. *In Procession Before the World: Martyrdom as Public Liturgy in Early Christianity*. Milwaukee: Marquette University Press, 2001.

Žižek, Slavoj. *Iraq: The Borrowed Kettle*. New York: Verso, 2004.

———. *Living in the End Times*. New York: Verso, 2011.

Index

Made in the USA
Monee, IL
15 January 2023

25325568R20100